With Regards,
Sandy Achonjie

CODE BLUE 99!
- A Miraculous True Story!
SECOND EDITION

Sandy Acharjee

AuthorHouse™
1663 Liberty Drive
Bloomington, IN 47403
www.authorhouse.com
Phone: 1-800-839-8640

© *2011 Sandy Acharjee. All rights reserved.*

No part of this book may be reproduced, stored in a retrieval system, or transmitted by any means without the written permission of the author.

First published by AuthorHouse   3/21/2011

ISBN: 978-1-4567-4590-5 (sc)
ISBN: 978-1-4567-4589-9 (hc)
ISBN: 978-1-4567-4588-2 (e)

Library of Congress Control Number: 2011903040

Printed in the United States of America

Any people depicted in stock imagery provided by Thinkstock are models, and such images are being used for illustrative purposes only. Certain stock imagery © *Thinkstock.*

This book is printed on acid-free paper.

Because of the dynamic nature of the Internet, any web addresses or links contained in this book may have changed since publication and may no longer be valid. The views expressed in this work are solely those of the author and do not necessarily reflect the views of the publisher, and the publisher hereby disclaims any responsibility for them.

*This book is dedicated to my beloved wife
Jharna (Janet) Acharjee
in appreciation of her sincere dedication
and true companionship.*

EDITOR'S NOTES

I thoroughly believe that my participation in the publishing of this book as its editor was certainly part of God's plan. Let me explain.

During Sandy's hospitalization, my husband entered the emergency room of the same hospital with a possible heart condition. Upon discharge, we decided to pay a visit to Sandy to give him our best wishes. It was then that I met his wonderful wife and daughter. Little did we know how grave his condition was at that time. He certainly didn't look like himself. We only stayed for a short while, telling Sandy and his family that we will pray for his speedy recovery.

Interestingly, in August of 2007, I had the opportunity to visit India with my husband, which was a life's dream of mine. Although we saw many beautiful sites, we were also overwhelmed by the amount of poverty that existed in these wonderful cities.

Shortly thereafter, Sandy began writing his book, per The Lord's instruction. He asked me to try to draw what he had seen on his way to and at Heaven's Gate. However, instead of the drawings, I began editing the text. As I was doing so, because of the above two situations, I could picture in my mind both Sandy's grave illness and the poverty of which he spoke.

His experience is truly a miracle, and we should all heed the five directives he was given from The Lord to the best of our ability. I have included a few lines from Scripture, which attest to the promise of the great things in store for us. (Actually, these were taken from a book, "Promises for You," which was given to me by a dear friend in 2006 – I believe this was the beginning of God's plan for me in connection with this book.)

Tell the Truth
>   Love…rejoices with the truth (Corinthians 13:6)

Sin No More
>   If you pay attention to these Laws and are careful to follow them, then the Lord your God will keep His covenant of love with you, as He swore to your fore-fathers. (Deuteronomy 7:12)

Surrender Yourself Completely to Me
>   Be joyful always; pray continually; give thanks in all circumstances, for this is God's will for you in Christ Jesus. (Thessalonians 5:16-18)

Walk with Me
>   Since we live by the Spirit, let us keep in step with the Spirit. (Galatians 5:25)

Be Good to the Poor
>   He who is kind to the poor lends to the Lord, and He will reward him for what he has done. (Proverbs 19:17)

It has been a tremendous privilege to edit this miraculous book and an honor to be a friend of the author, a kind and true "gift from God." All who know him feel that God has chosen him specially to spread His word through this publication.

>   (I can be reached at MarilynNeale@aol.com.)

Acknowledgements

There are many people who truly helped me go through my crisis period, and, without their genuine support and help, I would not be in a position to complete this book today. I need to mention some of their names and sincerely thank them all for their dedication, support, care and love.

Before I mention any names, I must sincerely thank God for His love and mercy; for His kindness; for His loving conversation and guidance; for sending me back to the earth with some specific instructions; and for His assurance to see me again next time. Lord, please give me strength, courage, wisdom and guidance, so that I can complete my unfinished tasks prior to my next visit.

The very next person I must thank is my wife, Jharna (Janet). She has been with me in every step of my crisis period. She has been a true companion. She always tried to keep me cheered up, even though she herself was tired, nervous and scared. She spent many nights with me in the hospital, sometimes with no sleep or very little sleep. All I can say to my wife is that you are a real gem, and I have been fortunate to have you as my life partner. You have been with me in every step on this side of Heaven. You have witnessed everything from the start of the crisis to the end. While I was at the Gateway to the Kingdom of Heaven and enjoying the beautiful view of the Heaven, including a loving conversation with God there, you literally were going through the roughest time of your life, sometimes not knowing what to do. I am sorry for all the events and I sincerely thank you for everything that you did for me.

I also must thank all my immediate family members who took much time from their work and spent a considerable amount of time visiting me in the hospital and taking care of one another.

I also would like to thank all of the doctors, nurses, nursing assistants, patient care assistants and technicians who took care of me during the entire crisis period. I would like to name a few doctors for their total dedication.

They are: Dr. M. D., Dr. U. K., Dr. P. V., Dr. J. L., Dr. P. C., Dr. D. H., Dr. A. S., Dr. J. S., Dr. M. L., Dr. E. S., Dr. J. S, Dr. G. H, Dr. J. M., Dr. L. Q., Dr. R. G., Dr. R. F., Dr. P. A., Dr. K. P, Dr. B. E., Dr. S. C. and Dr. V. N.

Thank you all. Without your dedication and utmost care, I would not be able to get better again, standing on my feet and ultimately writing this book.

I need to thank all of the nurses and other health care teams at the Intensive Care Unit on the upper floor, as well as all the super nurses and other professionals at the Critical Care Unit of the CVICU. I can still remember a few of their names such as Kelly, Kristen, Julianne, Rita, Mary Jo, Bogusia, Cathy, Pat, etc, etc. Every one of them was outstanding. I remember a few of the support team members such as Missy and Dan. Especially, I need to thank Dan, who is a patient care assistant at the CVICU. Dan always went an extra mile out of his way in order to help me. I also need to thank Steve who is a R.N. at the CVICU. Steve was very helpful to me and to my wife. Steve worked very diligently to bring me back to life. Thanks to all of you. Please forgive me if I cannot remember all of your names.

I need to thank all my colleagues, my bosses, my friends, who always supported me throughout the crisis. Many of them visited me on a regular basis to show their supports. "A friend in need is a friend indeed." They are truly my friends. I need to mention some of their names.

They are Frank and Ann DiTomasso, Regis and Marilyn Minerd, Joe and Ann Marie Mezzina, Al Jerele, David Stech, Kelly Grudzinski, John Higgs, Ted and Marilyn Neale, Bud Koller and many others.

As far as encouraging me to start writing this book, a few people have continuously suggested that I do so. They are, George Cantley, Ted Neale and his wife, Marilyn Neale.

As far as from the start to completion of this book is concerned, one person has supported me the most. She is Marilyn Neale. She has spent many hours in reviewing and editing the texts; guiding me in every step; suggesting alternate words; and making several phone calls to potential publishers and other organizations.

Marilyn, you have been like a true sister to me. You were always keeping an eye for any potential pitfalls. Without your continued guidance and support, this book would not have been completed and published. Thank you very much.

Marilyn is gifted with the talents of being an excellent editor. Any of my readers needing any editorial services may contact her at MarilyNeale@aol.com

As far as selecting an appropriate name for the book is concerned, the credit goes to Vikas Anand of Gurgaon, India who suggested to me that I use this name. I came to know Vikas and his family in early 2006. Thank you, Vikas. You were always kind to me.

There are many others who encouraged me to write this book and helped me in various ways. I am thankful for their guidance and support. I apologize for not mentioning all of their names.

Sincerely,

Sandy Acharjee

Contents

Introduction	xv
Sudden Crisis In Life	1
Further Complications At ICU	7
Death Or Near Death Experiences	15
Journey To An Unknown Destination	21
Magnificent Beauty Of Heaven	23
Face To Face With God In Heaven	25
Loving God & The Narrow Door	29
Return To Earth At Critical Care Unit	33
Readjustment After Return	35
Beginning Of A Miraculous Recovery	39
Recollection Of Events	47
Gangrenous Gall Bladder	51
Mini Surgery & Oxygen Therapy	55
Major Lung Surgery	59
Amazing Bounce Back To Life	67
Unexpected Apology From Dr. X	71
Conversation With God	75
Release From The Hospital	87
Return To Regular Activities	91
Inspiration	93
Testimonials	*101*

Introduction

I have never written a book in my life thus far nor did I have any intention to write one at any time. I do not consider myself a scholar, since I am not one. I am just a typical ordinary person.

But I do consider myself a strong family-oriented person, since my family has always been very important to me. I have always tried my best to fulfill my family's needs as much as possible. I always wanted the best for them within my means.

I have never been a strong religious person, abiding by any strict rules. However, I have always maintained good moral values to myself and my family. I was born a Hindu, and my father was always a very strong orthodox Hindu. He was a well renowned Sanskrit scholar, as well as a part-time Hindu priest. I did not step into my father's profession. I chose a different career path.

Although I myself was never a strong religious follower of any faith, I always believed in the existence of God from my childhood.

As a student, I quickly understood that nothing in the world just happened on its own. Nothing comes into existence unless someone makes it or someone somehow is responsible for the action.

For example, each and every person in the whole world, we did not come on our own. Our parents had to create us. Look at the three basic necessities for our survival - we need food, shelter and clothes to survive. Do they come on their own? They do not come on their own - someone had to make them. We live in some form of dwelling - they do not come on their own. Many people are behind the creation before we can live in our dwelling. Our clothes do not come on their own - someone had to create them. In the same manner, we can look at everything in the whole world, and we will find that nothing came on its own - Someone is or was responsible behind its creation.

I became a manufacturing engineer by profession. Throughout my career, my job basically was to create more complex, precise, challenging, and various shaped components. And at the end, when I looked at the final product, I asked myself - "How did they get here? Did they come on their own?" Of course not - there were many "creators" behind them.

My childhood belief in the existence of God at some point changed to the status of God as a Creator, and I became convinced that nothing in the world came on its own. Someone had to create each and every item in the whole world. This earth, the beautiful mountains, the enormous ocean, the rain forests, the atmosphere, and the changing seasons (whatever we see or we do not see) all had to be created by Someone. They did not come on their own.

Beyond this earth, the sun, the moon, the planetary systems, the entire universe had to be created by a Master Creator.

In my profession, we always strive for three things: quality, craftsmanship and low cost. Whenever we create something, these three factors are always the common attributes. In my life thus far, I have traveled extensively throughout many parts of the world, and every time I see the magnificent creation work of the Master Creator, I am amazed by the superb quality and flawlessness of the master craftsmanship. I often wondered if there was the third factor - namely, the cost. The third factor is most likely only limited to us as human beings.

As I grew older, sometimes I would wonder about the purpose of our life here on earth. We are born; we live here for x number of years; and then suddenly one day we die. What happens after that? According to Hindu beliefs, we come back to this earth over and over again, until our soul is purified to the state that it can be united with the Divine Great Soul. Once that happens, we are permanently liberated from the revolving cycles of life and death. As I said earlier, I was never a strong religious person of any faith. Therefore, I never paid much attention to this subject, and life continued for me with normal up's and down's.

I had absolutely no clue what I had in store for a period of approximately six to eight weeks, starting on October 15, 2006. During this period, I went from a relatively healthy condition to my sudden death or near death condition, without any warning, coming right out of the blue. All the odds were against me for my survival or a slight reversal of the condition. There was no remedy available to cure the root problem. One after another my situations were getting further complicated, to the point that I had to experience my death or near death condition. It happened on October 21, 2006.

From the beginning of this trauma, I always felt that an Invisible Force was causing everything, and none of us had any control over the situation.

Then, quite unexpectedly, I met God in person at the Gateway to the Kingdom of Heaven.

Initially, I was tremendously nervous and shaky by seeing the huge, gigantic-sized figure of God. But soon I discovered how kind, how loving and a genuine friend He was.

I had a heart-to-heart conversation with God for some time. He graciously sent me back to the earth and asked me to complete my unfinished tasks until He sees me again.

This book is one of the unfinished tasks that He asked me to complete.

He asked me to write the Truth and share the Truth with everyone without any fear.

He also asked me not to keep one penny from the sales of this book for myself. Each and every penny earned from the sales of this book must be spent to help the poor.

This book is about my experience; how it started; how things happened; and how miraculously I bounced back to life again.

This is a true story, and the writing of this book is fully inspired by God Himself. I tried my best to write everything in its truest form. I felt His presence was guiding me whenever I was writing this book.

As I said earlier, I am not a scholar. I am strictly an average person. By the same token, I am also not a professional writer. I have never written a book in my life nor did I have any intention to write one now. I apologize to all my readers for any errors or mistakes found in this book.

Also, I am not a Theologian. I have never been a strong religious follower of any faith. If any of the contents of this book appears to be contrary to your belief, please forgive me – I sincerely apologize. It is not at all my intention to write against any faith or belief. Who am I to challenge any faith or question any belief or practice? I have no intention of doing that. However, knowingly or unknowingly, if any of the contents of this book are hurtful to you and are contrary to your religious beliefs or any religious group, I sincerely beg your forgiveness and I truly apologize.

I consider myself to be an extremely fortunate person to be able to eyewitness the Kingdom of Heaven; to find the one and only narrow Entry Door to Heaven; and to meet God in person. I am extremely thankful to God that He sent me back to the earth with some specific instructions and tasks.

It does not matter what religion or faith to which we belong. The truth is: there is One, and only One, God - the Master Craftsman, the Master Creator of the entire universe. It does not matter by what name we call Him. He remains the same as One and only Supreme Being.

He loves all of us equally. There is no reason for Him to love me any more than you. I have not done anything special for Him to deserve that favor.

Sudden Crisis In Life

The date was October 15, 2006 and the day was Sunday. As I arose from my bed in the morning, I looked through my bedroom window and I said to myself, "What a beautiful morning it is! The sun is shining and the temperature looks perfect for a typical fall day - not too cold, not too warm."

I kept thinking that it won't be long before the cold weather gets here; and we are not going to have very many days like this one before the winter sets in. Therefore, I decided to enjoy the day, starting with a healthy breakfast in company with my near and dear ones.

Little did I know about the outcome of that gorgeous morning with a healthy breakfast plan. The beautiful morning quickly turned into a hellish one, as one of my near and dear family members suddenly attacked another near and dear one for no apparent reason. I would not have believed it if it did not happen in front of my eyes. I always regarded all of my family members as loving, caring and understanding individuals. Frankly speaking, I was in a total shock.

This unexpected situation totally marred the morning, and its effect ruined the entire day causing undue heartaches for myself and my loved ones. Someday, I intend to write another book stressing the absolute necessity of peace and harmony within the family members. Lack of peace and harmony among the family members is undoubtedly destroying many families in our society. At the moment, not much is done to understand the root causes and to take positive remedial actions.

That particular day could have been one of the most enjoyed as well as cherished days in my life. But what we think and expect does not always seem to happen.

There is a saying, "Man proposes. God disposes." The most beautiful morning for me undoubtedly ended as one of the worst days in my life. It seemed that some invisible power was causing the events of the day, and I had no control over any of the situations that led one thing to another. I felt myself as someone totally helpless with absolutely no power.

However, time does not wait for anyone. The day passed, and soon the night fell. My beloved wife and I were deeply moved by the unexpected events of the day. Neither she nor I had any appetite for having food or drinks - we simply did not feel like eating anything for our dinners. But the next morning was Monday, and we arose early to go to work. Therefore, we had to eat something just to survive. After dinner, we went to bed, but both of us could not sleep for quite some time, since we were preoccupied with the events of the day.

I did not know exactly when I dozed off, but later in the night I woke up with a pain in my upper stomach and abdomen. This was a sharp pain, and I never had experienced a similar type of pain before. Considering the day was quite eventful, hectic and having an unwilling dinner that evening which might have caused the indigestion and, therefore, the pain. I took one Rolaids (Antacid) tablet with a glass of water. After a few minutes, the pain seemed to ease, and I went back to sleep again.

Next morning (October 16), I woke up as usual and prepared myself for work. My wife insisted that I make an appointment with a physician who is a specialist in internal organs to find out why I had the severe pain at night. I nodded and left home for work.

That morning, I called Dr. P. V.'s office. Dr. P. V. is an internal organs specialist whom I met a few months earlier. Dr. P. V.'s secretary kindly gave me an appointment for the early afternoon. After a general check-up, the doctor asked me to go to the nearest hospital lab next morning, since he arranged for an immediate ultra sound test of my liver, gall bladder, pancreas and duodenum. The doctor also advised me to check into the nearest hospital should the pain return.

The night of October 16, I did not have any pain. When I awoke in the morning of October 17, I said to myself, "Everything must be fine. The pain must have been caused due to stress and indigestion."

However, since I had an appointment for various lab tests in the morning I went straight to the nearest hospital lab and had all the tests done. I asked the lab technician when my test results would be known. The technician said that the results would be sent to Dr. P. V. in three to four days.

After completing the lab tests, I went back to my work. I did not feel anything unusual. I kept saying to myself, "Everything must be fine and the pain must have been from the indigestion. There could be nothing serious." But deep inside I was still curious to know the results of my ultra sound tests. I called Dr. P. V.'s office and asked if they would call me and let me know when they received the test results. They said, "It will take a few more days, and the doctor will definitely contact you."

I went home after work, had my dinner, briefly watched TV, played a few computer games, and went to bed around 10:30 PM.

Shortly before midnight on October 17, I awoke with a very severe pain in my upper stomach and abdomen. The pain was taking place in the same area as it happened a few nights earlier. I got up and took a Rolaids tablet, as I had done a few nights earlier. Last time, a few minutes after taking the Rolaids, I was feeling better. This time, it was just the opposite. My pain was going to the extreme. It felt as if someone was stabbing me with a sharp knife over and over. It was beyond description. As the night was progressing, so was my pain worsening. I could not control myself and started to moan and groan.

My unexplained moaning and groaning awoke my wife. She tried to calm me down, but the pain was going far beyond my tolerance level. I felt my heart was racing and had an irregular beat. I could not lie down; I could not sit down; I could not stand up - what a terrible situation! I felt the pain was now spreading towards my chest.

My breathing was getting very irregular, and I was sweating profusely. By this time, it felt as if someone had changed the knife from a small one to a large one and started stabbing me left and right with the larger knife. I've never experienced anything like this in my life. Neither could I imagine that a pain of this type ever existed.

The time was a few minutes past 2 AM (October 18, early morning). By then, both my wife and I were beginning to wonder if I was having a heart attack. We knew whatever was happening, it was quite serious, and it required immediate medical attention. We grabbed the phone and desperately dialed 911 for immediate help. As the minutes passed, my condition was worsening. At this time, I found it very difficult to breathe, although I could hear the siren of the ambulance from a distance speeding towards its destination. The siren stopped as the ambulance parked in front of our house.

Quite hastily, two members of the paramedics came in the house and transferred me from my house to the ambulance. They found my pulse rate was abnormally high. My blood pressure was also dangerously high. They gave me a number of baby aspirins and asked me to swallow them. They also suspected that I was most likely having a heart attack.

The nearest hospital from my house is approximately five miles away. The paramedics called the Emergency Department of the hospital and advised them of my condition. They asked my wife to join them. One member of the paramedics was monitoring my condition during the transit, while the other drove the vehicle.

As soon as the ambulance pulled into the emergency area, they rapidly admitted me and put me in the Intensive Care Unit. The date of admittance was October 18, 2006, and the local time was approximately 3 AM.

Further Complications At ICU

In the hospital, I was immediately given an I.V. Soon I was put on the breathing machine. I was also hooked up to the vital monitoring system. I was told to lie down at all times, not to get up for any reason since my pulse rate was extremely high.

The nurse said that they would schedule various tests as soon as the doctors arrive in the morning. She said that the doctors had been alerted of my condition. My family physician, Dr. M. D., is also associated with this hospital and he comes here on a regular basis.

I must wait until the doctors arrive to find out what is happening with me. My wife, who accompanied me to the hospital, said she would stay until the doctors arrived. She kept me a good company. I looked at the room. This room is shared with another patient, who was awake. He told me his name, but I cannot remember now. I asked him what brought him to the hospital. I believe he said something to do with his breathing, possibly pneumonia, but I'm not sure today what he said exactly. All I remember is that he was to be released that day, and he was anxious to go home. He had been in the hospital for a number of days.

Soon the daylight was breaking, and it was time for shift change. New faces started to come in and introduce themselves. The lab technician came in to draw blood; patient care assistants came in to do the routine vital checks; and there were others.

I'm not sure if I was given some pain killers or not. My pain was still there, but, it was not as fatal as before. There were also a number of other people coming in and checking me, practically asking me the same questions over and over. I never met them before; therefore, I did not know who they were.

Soon Dr. M. D. came to see me. Dr. M. D. has been my family physician ever since he started his practice in Ohio. I was so happy to see him. He asked me all sorts of questions. He said that they did not know what was wrong with me. They would perform a variety of tests, including CT scan, MRI, blood tests, x-rays, etc., to determine the cause. My wife said that I had done the ultra sound tests in the same hospital just a day earlier, and we were still waiting to know the results. Dr. M. D. said that he would look into it. He started to check me with his stethoscope and I could tell from his face that he was deeply concerned. He said my pulse rate was extremely high, and I must not get up for any reason. As he left the room, he said he would be back as soon as the diagnosis was completed. That was Wednesday, October 18, 2006.

I was taken downstairs to various labs for several tests, including a CT scan. My wife accompanied me everywhere. I asked her to go home and rest for awhile, but she refused. She said that she would not be able to rest at home leaving me in this situation, since she would be worried about the outcome.

It was a busy day as I was undergoing various types of tests. There were also other doctors who were coming in and asking me various questions. The day passed with tests and anxieties. I still did not know what was wrong with me.

My daughter came to visit me in the evening. When the visiting hours were over, I insisted that my wife go home and rest for awhile. Otherwise, both of us would be in the hospital. It was hard enough just to have one person being sick. If both of us became sick, the situation would be totally out of control. She went home reluctantly and said that she would be back in the morning.

After my wife and daughter went home, I noticed that my roommate was still there. I mentioned to him that I thought he would be going home that day. He said that he would be released the next day. We chatted for awhile, and I dozed off at some point.

Whether I dozed off due to exhaustion or medication, I do not know. I kept waking up as the technicians came to draw blood, check on vitals or check my blood sugar level, since I am diabetic. They did not care whether I was asleep or awake. They had to attend to their duties.

However, these interruptions kept me from sleeping. Once the sleep was interrupted, it was difficult to sleep again. Even when I managed to sleep again, there was the next interruption - breathing therapy. I had to do the therapy three or four times a day until the medication depleted each time. It usually took about 15 minutes to deplete the medication. Then there were the breathing exercises - I had to do it four or five times per day. I am not complaining as I know all these treatments are absolutely necessary and, without these treatments, a patient in my condition cannot get better.

The night passed on. Now, it was Thursday, October 19, 2006. My wife could not sleep well at home because of the anxieties. She came to see me early morning. My daughter dropped her to the hospital on her way to work that morning. The situation did not change. We still did not know what was happening to me. Routine tests and diagnosis continued.

I cannot remember what time it was when Dr. M. D. came to see me. He said that he had some good news and some bad news. The good news is that they know what is happening, but the bad news is they cannot do anything to rectify it. I asked him to elaborate the good news. He said that I had a severe gall bladder attack. During the attack, several gall stones ruptured, and it appeared that they ruptured with a tremendous force. A few stones penetrated the nearby organ, pancreas, and went from one end to the other. The pancreas was punctured, and that was making the heart work overtime, resulting in an extremely high pulse rate condition.

He said, "The situation is very serious." He also added, "In medical terms, it is called pancreatic, but, in your case, you have the pancreas that is severely wounded and damaged. A situation that is not normal."

I asked Dr. M. D., if anything can be done to rectify the problem, and he said to me, "That is the bad news. We can remove the gall bladder surgically, but we cannot proceed until your pulse rate normalizes.

The doctor continued, "Your pulse rate will not be normalized until the pancreas is healed."

The doctor paused for a moment and continued, "This is the dilemma. There is absolutely nothing we can do about the damaged pancreas. As of now, there are no medications or surgical procedures available to repair the ruptured pancreas."

He continued, "Medical science can only do the pancreas transplant, but in your case that is also not feasible. First, we must find a donor organ, and then have the proper surgical condition."

I asked Dr. M. D., "What do you mean by proper surgical condition?"

The doctor said, "With the current heart rate condition that you have, we cannot even do a gall bladder removal operation. Gall bladder operation is considered to be a relatively simple operation. If we cannot do a simple gall bladder operation, how can we do a major pancreas transplant operation? It is very risky, and we will not do it."

Dr. M. D. stayed in the room a few more minutes and said he was sorry that medically nothing can be done to ease the situation. He said, "The only thing you can do is pray and hope for the condition to improve so that we can at least remove the gall bladder and possibly some stones."

He checked my vitals and left the room with instructions to the appropriate personnel for a 24-hour, around-the-clock intensive care services.

After Dr. M. D. left, both my wife and I were saddened to know the diagnosis. Both of us had been eagerly waiting to hear some positive news. Now, we knew what was wrong with me, but there were no solutions, no remedies.

How would the wounded pancreas get healed? I must be having internal bleeding due to the puncture of the pancreas by the penetrating gall stones. There were no medications to make me better, and the doctors could not do any surgical procedures.

How would I get better? Worries and concerns surrounded me. My roommate wished me well and left the hospital, since he was released. I kept thinking, "When would I be released? When would I be able to go home? Perhaps, that day would never come."

My wife kept cheering me up, giving me hope and saying, "Don't worry, everything will be ok." But deep inside, both she and I knew it would be a long time before everything would be ok, perhaps never.

I remember a number of doctors who started visiting me and checking my conditions with genuine concern. I also remember some of their names, Dr. P. V., Dr. U. K., Dr. V. N. and a few more. They basically said the same thing as Dr. M. D. had said to me earlier: they could not do anything until my pulse rate came down; the situation was pretty serious and they asked me to hang in.

My daughter came to visit me in the evening. I insisted that my wife go home and take some rest. I told her not to worry about me, and I'd be fine. She reluctantly left with mixed emotions. On one hand she knew the cause of my problems; on the other hand, she was very concerned to know that there was no remedy.

After she left, I felt the room was quieter than the night before. I realized that might be due to the departure of my roommate. I could not sleep. I kept thinking of the events of the day. I was still hoping that I might be able to go back to my normal life someday. But right now I could not see how it was possible. "The doctors will not even operate on my gall bladder to remove the ruptured stones. How will my wounded pancreas get healed?" I was desperately searching for a ray of hope, but I did not find any.

Needless to say, I did not sleep well that night, since I passed the night amidst anxieties, pain and uncertainties. The next morning was Friday, October 20, 2006. For some reason, I was finding it difficult to breathe, as if some heavy load was resting on my chest. As usual, my wife came in the early morning. She did not sleep well either. She was also concerned about the remedy or lack of remedy in this situation.

When the RN came to see me, I mentioned about my difficulty in breathing. The doctor was notified, and I was sent for more tests. When I was brought back to my room, I asked my wife if she would help me to the attached bathroom. I had been bed-ridden ever since I came to the hospital, and it would probably do me good to stand up. She hesitated and wanted to call the RN. I said not to bother them. "They are busy, and I'm not the only patient." She did not want to do that, since the doctor previously told me not to stand up. I told her I'd be fine. "Let's try." Reluctantly she helped me to stand up.

This was the first time I was standing since I was brought to the hospital. Actually, I felt proud of being able to stand again and being able to walk to the attached bathroom. I looked at the mirror in the bathroom - my beards were growing big, and I should shave my beards off. My wife said, "Don't bother. Let the beards grow."

At that time, I saw the floor RN came rushing into the room and speaking to me in an extremely angry voice. She wanted to know what exactly I was doing and why did I stand up. I tried to explain. She quickly placed me in my bed and said to me, "Absolutely no standing! It is an order!"

I asked her why she was doing this. She said that when I stood up in the bathroom, my pulse rate went so high that I could have collapsed any moment.

I asked her how she knew that. She said that she could monitor my heart rate from her office twenty four hours around the clock. She left the room asking my wife to keep an eye on me so that I did not stand up again.

That was the end of my adventure of standing up for a long time, but I was still feeling good being able to stand up, even though the duration was extremely short.

Later, I was advised by one of the doctors that the tests taken earlier that day indicated I had pneumonia. I asked the doctor what caused my pneumonia. The doctor said it was not uncommon to have pneumonia in the hospital, "It could be viral."

Having pneumonia was the reason I was having trouble breathing. The doctor said that I had some fluids in both of my lungs and it would take a few more tests to determine which lung needed to be drained first.

This news had shocked both me and my wife. Now, it seems to be one thing after another. This one is quite unexpected and out of the blue. However, breathing is a very basic need for survival. If we cannot breathe, we cannot live much longer.

My situation was getting more and more complex: first the ruptured gall stones, which are still floating; the surgeons are unable to do a simple surgery to remove the gall bladder and stones; a punctured and wounded pancreas that was still under shock and unable to do any remedial action for that; now the viral pneumonia, having fluids in both lungs and much difficulty in breathing. I was wondering, "What would be the next?"

I was taken downstairs for a few more tests, one of which was an MRI to determine the amount of fluid and its exact locations. I was advised that the doctor will perform a simple surgical procedure next day (Saturday, October 21, 2006) around noon. I would need to be brought down a little earlier so that the doctors could do a final review of the condition prior to the operation.

As usual, my daughter came to visit me in the evening. My wife went home reluctantly. I asked her to contact my son, who lived in the neighboring state of Michigan, and let him know of this new development.

After my wife left, I felt very sad and anxious. I kept thinking, "I did not come to the hospital for this treatment. I came here to find out and fix the cause of my original pains."

The doctors had been saying that they could not do anything about my original problem, and now I was going to be treated for pneumonia that I did not have when I came to the hospital. It seemed that the odds were against me. An unknown force had taken control of my destiny, and I was totally helpless.

But my wife kept cheering me up; she continued to encourage me. She said, "We must go with what the doctors are saying. The doctors know better, and they are here to make the patients better."

Death Or Near Death Experiences

The night passed. It was now Saturday, October 21, 2006. I dozed off a few times throughout the night, and every time I woke up whenever the routine check-up people were conducting their duties. As usual, my wife came in the morning. She did not sleep well also.

I was taken down a little earlier than the scheduled time for my fluid draining operation. I was brought down to the MRI lab where the procedure was going to take place. My wife came along.

I sat on a bed exposing my back towards the MRI technician. The attending RN explained the procedure to me - they were going to drain the fluid out of my left lung. The doctor, who was going to perform the surgical procedure, was Dr. X. He came in and put a needle on my left back. He said that it would take a few minutes before the needle would locally numb the area and he would be back in a few minutes.

I noticed that there seemed to be a little difference of opinion between the nurse, the MRI technician and the doctor with the amount of fluid or its exact location. I was not able to find out what exactly was the cause for the difference of opinion.

The doctor took his time to return to the lab. When he came, he took a long needle and penetrated it through the back into my lungs. I immediately felt pain during the procedure and asked the RN if it was supposed to hurt? She and the doctor said, "A little." But to me it seemed to hurt more than a little.

I could not see my back. My wife later said there was hardly any fluid that came out. It was a very little amount of fluid mixed with blood. After the procedure, they took me next door for an x-ray and sent me upstairs.

I knew something was terribly wrong, as I started to feel extremely unwell immediately after the operation. But I did not know exactly what was wrong with me. I asked the attending RN if my post operation x-ray was normal. She said to me, "Everything is fine."

Once I was taken back up to my room, I saw that my son, my daughter-in-law and my granddaughter were waiting for me there. I was very happy to see them. The last time I saw them was on the previous Sunday, October 15, 2006.

I believe by then the time was shortly after 1 PM. This was the first time I noticed that, deep inside me, an inner voice started telling me that my life was coming to an end very soon, probably in less than 30 to 45 minutes. The inner voice continued to warn me, as my departure time from this world was getting near by the minutes.

I kept thinking that it takes usually over three hours by car from my son's place to the hospital. I asked him if they had lunch.

They said, "No."

I told them to go and have something quick in the cafeteria downstairs, for two reasons, one that the cafeteria stops serving lunch at 1:30 PM. The other was I felt tired and I needed to take a few minutes rest. I also told them not to delay in returning, as I needed to see them back as soon as possible.

They complied and went downstairs. My wife also went with them. Up until now, my wife was trying to cope with all the difficult situations by herself. Seeing my son, my daughter-in-law and my granddaughter there gave her some strength and moral support that she needed very badly.

But the real truth of my sending them away was that I knew my life was coming to an end very soon. If something happened in the next few minutes, they probably would remain hungry without food, as they would have no appetite for food should I pass away. I did not want them to stay hungry after a long drive from their home.

I was feeling weaker by the minute. The inner voice continued to tell me, "Your life is over, only a few more minutes left for you to live."

I was anxiously waiting for my loved ones to return to the room. I did not want to depart from this world without saying farewell to them.

Around that time, they returned to the room and saw me awake. They were asking if I slept a little or not. I told them, "Listen, I need to tell you something. I've only a few more minutes to live in this world. There is something terribly wrong with me."

My wife and my son said, "Don't say anything like this. You will be fine. Everything will be ok."

I said to them, "I do not have much time. Let me say it before it is too late. These are the final moments of my life."

I begged them to live peacefully and in harmony after my departure. I asked them to take care of each other. I blessed them with my final blessings and wished them well.

At that point, I looked at my wife, and I took her hand in mine. I said to her, "I might not have been an easy person to live with for all these years we had been together. Please forgive me for any and all of my wrong doings."

I continued to say that I loved her, and I loved the family dearly, and I was sorry to leave her in this manner. I repeatedly urged all of them to live in peace and in harmony. I blessed them all.

My wife and son still did not realize what I was trying to say. They kept on saying, "You'll be fine! Why are you saying such things? You'll be fine!" I told them again, "Listen, I only have a few moments of my life left. Good bye to all of you, and God bless you! Love one another and stay in peace."

My wife looked at me, and, for the first time since the beginning of this trauma, I saw tears in her eyes. She realized that I was serious and not joking. Whatever I was saying was genuine and urgent. She said to me, "You cannot leave me like this alone."

I said, "I'm sorry. I didn't plan it this way either. But the time has come for me to say Goodbye! I love you!" I touched her forehead and tendered my final blessings!

Within a few seconds, I collapsed on the bed and they said later to me that my body was getting stiff. My wife didn't know what to do or say. The entire episode was so sudden and unexpected, that it did not sink in for a few moments.

Either she or my son pushed the emergency call button for help. The RN for that floor rushed into the room, and she was shocked to see me die that quickly.

She realized what was going on. She immediately declared, "*Code Blue! Room #___*" on me and asked for the Emergency Response Team to rush into that Room. Later I found out that the "*Code Blue or Code 99*" is a secret code used by the hospital to alert the Emergency Response Team that someone is passing away or just passed away.

After I collapsed, I felt all my senses were disappearing one by one very quickly. First, I lost my visual sense - I could not see anyone. I was talking to them a few moments earlier. Now I could not talk. My wife was holding my hand. Very soon, I lost the sense of touch. I lost the other senses, as well. But I felt that my sense of hearing was still there for some time. Several minutes after collapsing, I was still able to hear what was being said in the room.

If I may offer a suggestion to my readers at this point, please do not say any negative words or comments at the time of someone's death. You may think he or she is dead and what you are saying he or she cannot hear. You'll be surprised to know that the sense of hearing is the last one that departs at the time of death. You do not want to make comments or say something that you would not normally say in front of the person if the person was alive.

In my case, I could not see, I could not feel the touch, I could not smell or I could not speak, but I continued to hear the noises of several medical professionals rushing into the room, asking everyone to leave the room in a hurry. They were trying very hard to revive me, but, by their words, I could sense that they were not succeeding. I heard one doctor saying, "We are rapidly losing him" and another doctor said, "He is not responding at all. We just lost him!"

These are the last words that I could remember. I could hear them no more. All my senses seemed to fade away. Everything was quiet. I fell into a deep eternal sleep.

Journey To An Unknown Destination

For a moment, I felt like, "I do not belong to this world any more. I need to depart from here. My world is gone. I could see my body lying flat on the hospital bed. But I felt there was no reason for me to stay here any more."

For some reasons, I felt like my brain was still functioning for the analytical or reasoning point of view because I was wondering, "What do I do now? Where do I go from here? I'm no longer a part of this world."

As I was wondering, suddenly a bright Light appeared before me. The Light was extremely bright and sharp.

As soon as I saw the Light, I knew it appeared before me with superior authority. I knew, "It means business and I better obey it. One little thought of disobeying it will be very fatal."

The Light kept a safe distance from me. Then, the Light became very bright. Due to its extreme brightness, everything disappeared from me. I could not see a thing any more, other than the bright Light. The only thing I could do was to obey Its command. The Light started to pull me, and I was to follow the Light. I noticed the Light was pulling me like a magnet pulls the metal. I've absolutely no control over anything. My job was to follow the Light wherever It wants to take me.

I started to follow the Light, keeping the safe distance. The Light was bright and scary at first, but now I felt its mission was to protect me and guide me throughout the journey to my unknown destination.

I remember following the Light, traveling at a very fast speed, faster than anything I knew. During the journey, I began to like the Light as It was protecting me.

I found the Light to be soothing. I remember passing through some black holes like big round tunnels at tremendous speed. Together, we traveled for quite some time. Exactly how long, I do not know.

After a long journey, suddenly the Light stopped, and I had to stop. If one is following a speedy car on the highway and, if the car ahead stops all of a sudden, the car behind must stop. It was a similar situation. I was following the Light, and, when It stopped, I had to stop. When the Light stopped, It was still looking at me, and I was looking at Him, as well. I was wondering, "Why did the Light stop moving? What do I do now?"

I kept on gazing at the Light from a safe distance. To me, the distance between the Light and me seemed to be a several thousand feet away.

I noticed that the Light was still gazing at me, as if it was keeping an eye on me for every move I would make.

At that point, I was beginning to wonder, "Where am I? What is this place? What's behind the Light? Why is the Light not moving? Why did it stop?"

Magnificent Beauty Of Heaven

Up until now, I couldn't see anything besides the Light. The Light was so bright, and I had been gazing at it for a considerable length of time.

Nothing else was visible to me.

Gradually, the area where the Light was situated was beginning to clear for me. For the first time, I was seeing that the Light stopped inside a large compound that was fenced in with very high and extraordinarily beautiful fences.

Slowly, I could see the entire area as far as I could see. The area was fenced in from all four sides. The area inside the fences was the most beautiful large compound I had ever seen in my life.

Nothing in this world could ever come close to the beauty of this place. The fences were tall, but they were magnificent. I was so taken by the beauty of the place inside, that I could not keep my eyes away from it. The more I saw the more curious I became, and I wanted to see more.

The brightness of the Light did not blind me any longer, rather It was shining upon the entire compound with a soothing light similar to the moon light on a full moon night only several times brighter. Because of the soothing Light shining upon the area I started to see the entire area of this huge compound very clearly.

I saw, there were many marvelous big buildings after buildings. Big buildings would be an understatement. I should say, they were mansions after mansions, and they were so gorgeous and so beautiful.

The mansions were very large in size, their structures were superb, and their roofs were of a bright golden color. Some of the mansions also had bright copper colored roofs. I've not seen anything like these mansions anywhere in the world. Throughout my life, I've traveled extensively to many countries. But the beauty of this place was unique, unlike any other beautiful places I've ever seen. Its beauty was awesome and beyond description.

I could not turn my eyes away from this magnificent place. The more I saw, the more I was getting stunningly astonished. I wanted to go inside the fences. "Where are the entrance ways to this place?" I asked myself.

I continually searched for an Entrance Way, all around the perimeters as far as I could see, but I could not find one.

Face To Face With God In Heaven

I was wondering how I could go across the beautiful fences into the magnificent compound. I started to look all around the fences as far as I could see. I was searching for at least one entrance way to this compound. I was shocked when I noticed that the entire complex was fenced in and there was not a single entrance way that I could see anywhere throughout the perimeters as far as I could see.

The entire boundary was well protected by the Angel like figures. Nobody could even dare intrude into the place. I started to look all around the perimeters again and again. Alas, there was not a single entry or gate anywhere in sight!

I was quite disappointed not finding any gate or entrance way into this place. I started to look deeper into the compound, and I could see many Angel-like figures floating. I saw from a distance some human-like beings who could either walk or float.

The entire area inside the compound looked so peaceful and so calm that I instantly fell in love with this place. I kept thinking, "How do I get into this beautiful place? There has to be an Entrance somewhere. Where is the Entrance? How can I find the Entrance?"

As I was desperately searching for the Entrance, I noticed my companion Light was still looking at me and watching me for every move I was going to make.

Not finding an Entrance into this place, I felt sad. My focus, by then, had shifted from the inside of the beautiful compound to the place where I was standing. Suddenly, I started to wonder, "Where am I? What is this place?"

It felt like I was standing somewhere. All of my attention thus far was focused on the inside and the perimeter of the fences all around the magnificent compound. At that time I was beginning to wonder, "What is this place upon which I'm standing?" My focus now shifted to the area where I was standing.

I noticed I was standing on a platform. I also noticed that I was standing at the extreme far left-hand corner, almost to the edge of this platform. For the first time, I realized that the Light I followed all along was now situated inside the beautiful compound, and I was standing on a platform outside the compound. I also noticed that the platform was rather large (approximately 1000 feet long), and it was located at a high altitude. And there I was – at the edge, extreme far left corner of the platform.

"Why does this platform have no railings?" I was wondering, "I'm standing so close to the edge, what if I fall off the edge?"

Being curious, I looked downwards on my left from that edge, and what I saw was the most dreadful scene of my life. If I fell off the edge, I would fall thousands of miles deep into an unknown scary world. That fall definitely would be the end of my life. I could not ever imagine where I would fall to. Only God knows where I'd fall.

Just the mere thought of the fall was so scary and so frightening that I instantly moved a few steps away from the extreme edge.

I looked at my companion Light one more time, and I noticed the Light was carefully watching me and my every move.

At that point I just realized that the magnificent place I was looking at all along was nothing but the Kingdom of Heaven, and I was standing outside the Kingdom of Heaven on a platform or an altar. As I could see some Angels and some human like persons inside the compound, I desperately started to look at their faces to see if I could see a familiar face, such as my mother or my father or someone else whom I know. I could not see anyone. I was quite disappointed by not seeing any familiar faces.

I now decided to survey the altar where I was standing at the extreme far left corner. There was no other person on the altar at the time; I was the only one.

For the first time, I started to look towards my front. The altar was approximately 200' feet wide. I noticed, at the end, towards the center, there were three big steps. Each step was about five to seven feet high, with the same depth. On top of the second step, the third step had approximately 20 to 30 feet depth and no height to it. Behind that there was a wall that was approximately 70 feet high. This back wall adjoined the boundary fences that I was looking at earlier.

I started to look from there towards my right. As I mentioned earlier, the altar was approximately 1000' feet long. As I was looking towards the center of this high walled platform, my eyes were struck in awe at what I saw. At the center of that location there was a huge throne. Lo and behold! There was the Lord! The Lord was sitting on the throne!

Loving God & The Narrow Door

As soon as I saw Him, I knew He was the Supreme Lord! I started to tremble with fear! He was so huge. Here, I am 5'6" tall standing at the extreme far left corner and looking at the center of that altar, and He was approximately 600 feet away from me. He was sitting on the throne, and at that sitting position He appeared to be approximately 35 to 40 feet tall. Therefore, when He stands up, I presume, He would be about 70 feet tall. He was very well proportioned and wore a white robe.

Seeing his huge, gigantic appearance I again started to tremble with fear. My knees felt very weak. I was standing at the extreme far edge of the platform, and I could very easily fall off the edge with my fearful trembling. He was such a powerful, overwhelming and mesmerizing figure that I could not look at Him for too long. I was trembling with fear so much thinking that this would be the end of my life. The Lord will not spare me.

I could not look at Him straight at His face. I was so afraid. I started to look slightly towards the left of the throne (right from my position) and I was totally amazed to discover a very narrow door. The door was so narrow that it struck me as completely out of proportion.

I now realized that this narrow door is the only entrance to the inside of the Kingdom of Heaven. This is the only entrance in the entire perimeter of the compound. This is the entrance I had been desperately searching for a bit earlier.

"How can I go through this door?" I asked myself. The Lord is so big and frightening. He is sitting near the door. I cannot dare myself to go near the door. It was quite evident to me that I could not even try to enter through the door unless the Lord allowed me to go through the door.

It had been pretty clear to me that I was now standing at the Gate to the Kingdom of Heaven and I was completely at the mercy of the Lord. I was still nervous and shaky. But then the Lord spoke to me. He has a very deep, commanding voice, but, at the same time, I noticed His voice was also a loving one.

Language did not seem to be a barrier at all. When the Lord spoke, I could understand that in any of the languages that I know. By the same token, it didn't matter in which language I responded, the Lord understood every word even before I spoke.

The Lord looked at me and asked, "What are you doing here?"

I shrugged my shoulder, meaning, "I do not know."

He said to me in an authoritative, but loving, voice, "Your time has not come yet. I'm sending you back to the earth. Go back until your time comes."

By then, I gathered some courage, as I noticed I was not shaking any longer with fear. The Lord continued, "Go back and complete your unfinished tasks. Love your family. Love your children. Pay attention to your daughter. She needs your help."

Hearing the loving and caring voice of the Lord, I gathered a little more courage, and I asked, "Lord! I'm not worthy of standing before You. I'm a sinner! I've sinned, Lord! How can I be sure that I can enter through this door next time? And, Lord, please tell me - when will be my next time?"

The Lord did not respond.

I continued to plead, "Lord! Please provide me with some guidance. How can I prepare myself for the next time? How can I make myself worthy of standing before you next time? And, I do not know how much time I'll have before the next time."

The Lord still did not respond.

I continued pleading, "Please Lord! Please guide me to prepare myself for next time. Please tell me if I need to join any church, any temple, any synagogue, any religious institute, any religious association or any other place. I'll do whatever You say, but please guide me."

The Lord looked at me and said, "No, it is not necessary for you to join any church, any temple or anything else. Those things are not important to Me."

(Although the Lord indicated to me that membership to any religious group is not necessary to enter the Kingdom of Heaven, we, as humans, definitely need a support group to help us through our difficult times, remind us of the importance of worshiping God, teach us in the Ways of the Lord, and assist us in accomplishing His directives.)

The Lord continued, "What is important to Me is your personal relationship with Me, how sincere, how honest, how true are you with Me? That's the only thing that counts."

I looked at the Lord and begged Him to be merciful to me. I said, "Lord! I am a human being. When I go back, I'll be involved with my day-to-day activities, and I'll be back to my worldly life. Please, Lord! Please give me some specific instructions or guidelines that I can follow."

The Lord looked at me and said, "Here are some instructions for you. I want you to follow them between now and your next time."

He gave me five instructions and asked me to go back to the earth until He sees me again next time.

I will elaborate on His instructions to me towards the final chapter of this book. In the mean time, I'm now back to the earth, and let me explain my experiences back here.

Return To Earth At Critical Care Unit

I believe it was Tuesday, October 24, 2006, when I finally opened my eyes (first time since I departed from this earth on previous Saturday, October 21, 2006). I cannot remember the exact time, but I remember when I opened my eyes I saw a loving motherly- type nurse sitting beside me and looking at me. When she saw me opening my eyes, she exclaimed with joy, "There you are! You finally opened your eyes. We all are anxiously waiting for you!"

I asked her, "Where am I? What is this place?"

She said to me in a loving voice, "It is a long story, my dear. Thank God! You finally opened your eyes. You have been terribly sick. We are all working hard day and night to bring you back."

I asked the motherly lady, "How did I get here?" I told her I was there with God a few moments earlier. He was talking to me, and He said to me, "I am sending you back to the earth."

She said to me, "I believe you, but for now let me go and tell all the doctors and the nurses that you have opened your eyes. Oh! They will be so happy to hear that. They are anxiously waiting for this news. It is a miracle!"

The loving motherly type nurse left the room, and I dozed off again. Even though I was asleep, I could hear the footsteps of several people coming into my room. I think they were looking at my vitals, monitoring the numbers on the life support machine, and discussing the results among themselves. I could sense from their expressions that they were full of excitement and joy.

I was dozing off and on quite frequently that day. It did not matter whether I opened or closed my eyes, I could not stop remembering every moment of my experience at the Gateway to the Kingdom of Heaven. I was so taken by the awesome beauty of the Kingdom of Heaven, that I could not keep my mind off the place where I was a few moments earlier. God's instructions to me were ringing back in my ears over and over. His final words to me were, "I'm sending you back to the earth until I see you again next time."

Readjustment After Return

It seemed to me that all of my prior experiences in this world were totally blanked out of my mind. I could not remember anything in this world, at least for the first one or two days after my return. I was somewhat disoriented definitely the first day of my return, and my recollection of events might be slightly out of sequence. However, I do remember a few major events. Let me explain those events as I remember.

Between my frequent sleepy periods, I remember once seeing my wife who was holding my hand. I looked at her, and her face definitely looked familiar. A few moments later, I could recognize her as my wife.

She asked me if I could remember anything. I shook my head indicating, "No." I saw tears in her eyes, but these tears did not appear to be tears of her sorrow. I knew these tears were reflecting her joy. She said, "Thank God! You are back! You went away, and I was so nervous, I did not know what to do."

For the first time I noticed that I could not speak. I had no voice. She was holding a clipboard and I managed to scribble. "What happened to me? Where am I? What is this place? What am I doing here?"

She asked, "Can't you remember what happened to you last Saturday?"

I wrote, "No. What happened to me?"

She said, "After you collapsed in the Intensive Care Unit room upstairs the Emergency Response Team rushed into the room and drove us away from the room in a hurry. They tried to revive you there but they failed to bring you back to life. They were there for a very long time. We were not allowed to see what they were doing. However, some doctors decided to put you on artificial life support machine and transfer you to the Critical Care Unit with twenty-four-hour/around-the- clock care."

She continued, "This is called the Critical Care Unit of this hospital. A lot of doctors and nurses have been working very hard for the last three days to bring you back to your consciousness." She paused.

I was trying to concentrate and remember any events that took place last Saturday. I could vaguely remember that I was at the Intensive Care room when I collapsed.

My mind was still occupied with the experience that I encountered outside this world. I could remember every second of my journey, every moment of my being there, but I could not remember anything that transpired here in this hospital for the last three days.

As my wife was having discussions with me, I noticed that my hands and legs were restrained to the bed. I could not move them too much. I also noticed that I was breathing through a large diameter clear plastic hose.

I wrote on the clip board. "Why are my hands and legs tied to the bed? Why am I breathing through the plastic hoses?"

She said, "Your hands and legs are restrained for your own safety so that you could not pull any of the pipes out of your body. Pulling any of the hoses or pipes could prove to be very fatal."

I wrote. "Did you say pipes? How many pipes are there?"

Before she answered I remember a nurse came into my room and asked me to take it easy. She did not want me to get over exhausted. She did not want me to get excited as it might put undue stress to my respiratory system.

My wife asked the nurse, "He wants to know how many pipes are attached to his body and what are they for."

The nurse said, "Quite a few."

She pointed her finger to one of them and said, "This large diameter hose is for your breathing. It is tied to the artificial breathing machine. All your breathing is taking place through this machine."

She continued, "You have three tubes coming off the left side of your chest. They are called drain tubes."

She said, "You have another one coming off a little below, and it is called Catheter. That is to protect your kidney."

The nurse continued, "You have intra-venous tubes feeding your body with the necessary fluids and nutrition. You also have a tube for blood transfusion."

My wife commented, "Pulling any of the tubes off your body will be disastrous. That's why they tied your hand and body."

The nurse said, "You have not been a good boy. You were trying to pull them off in your sleep. Perhaps, you didn't even know that. Now that you are awake and if you promise to behave, we can arrange to get you off the artificial breathing."

Beginning Of A Miraculous Recovery

I did not realize what the nurse meant about my artificial breathing, not until I met a couple of professional healthcare personnel who entered into my room. I cannot remember what day it was. Was it the same day or the day after? I cannot remember.

However, they said to me that they were going to replace my artificial breathing tube with my own breathing tube. They explained the procedure - how they were going to do that. I did not fully understand.

They continued to explain that, during the emergency last Saturday, the doctors had to pop my lung tubes open and replaced it with the artificial breathing tube. Now the time has come to reverse the situation.

I was extremely shocked to know that my lung tubes could be popped open.

"How is that possible? How can that come out of my throat?" I was wondering.

One of the nurses brought my own lung tube in a tray and showed it to me. "Take a look! This is your own," she said. I looked at it and it looked fairly long. I wondered how did this pop out?

"If you put that in my throat, I'm going to be choked," I wrote on the clip board.

They said, "Don't worry. It came out of there ok, and it should go back there ok. First few minutes you will feel uncomfortable, but after a few minutes longer you will feel much better. There is nothing better than your own breathing tube. You will feel much better soon after replacement."

I wrote, "Where was my breathing tube kept all this time? Where did you get it from?"

One of the nurses said it was in the fridge all this time.

I watched them how efficiently they replaced the tubes. It didn't take that long. Initially, my throat felt irritated, but then it calmed down. I was not allowed to talk for some time. Even though I got my own tubes back, they still kept me on oxygen supply through my nose. By the time, they completed their tasks, I felt exhausted and fell asleep again.

I remember seeing my wife sitting beside me a few times. She told me that she never felt so helpless like this before. My sudden departure from this earth was a total shock to her. It was completely unexpected.

As she was having a light discussion, I remember a couple of doctors who came to visit me that day. One was our family physician, Dr. M. D. He has been a well-respected physician at this hospital. He checked my pulse and looked at the chart.

He said, "Your condition is still very unstable. All of the problems you had earlier are still there. How do you feel now?"

I did not know how to respond to his question. I simply did not know how I felt. The doctor left the room saying that he would be back again.

After the doctor left the room my wife continued to lament, "See, the danger period is not over yet. Anything still could happen to you. You cannot leave us alone. We need you."

Somehow I managed to tell her briefly that I was at the Gateway to the Kingdom of Heaven, and I met God. God said to me, "I am sending you back to the earth."

She said to me, "I will listen to it later. Don't talk too much now. The nurse told you not to get over exhausted."

I remember another doctor who visited me that day. His name was Dr. P. C. He came to check if I was making any progress. He was the designated surgeon, who would be doing the gall bladder surgery, and he would also like to probe if there were any ruptured stones in the vicinity.

He said that he would come to check my status almost daily so that he could assign a date and time for my gall bladder operation.

He also said that several tests would be required prior to his establishing the date and time.

He mentioned several tests, but I remember one of them was a nuclear test that I had to take within the next few days prior to the surgery. After checking my chart Dr. P. C. left.

I remember Dr. P. V. also visited me that day, keeping an eye on my status.

Soon the night fell, and the visiting hours ended. My wife had left for home. I had slept off and on throughout the night.

Next morning was Wednesday, October 25. A female doctor came in and introduced herself as Dr. E. S. She said that she was in charge of the infectious disease control. She would visit me on a regular basis, and I should not hesitate to contact her anytime, if there was a need.

As usual, Dr. M. D. came to check my status. He said that I would be going through a series of tests for them to find out the exact status of my gall bladder and a few other organs. Dr. M. D. mentioned that, although my condition was slightly better than the previous day, the condition would need to get more stabilized prior to confirming a date for my gall bladder surgery.

Dr. P. C. also came, and he expressed hope that a surgery can be scheduled soon, if the progress continues in the same manner. He said that he would be back again the next day.

I believe it was the same day when I had a number of my colleagues who came to visit me. I remember a few names: Ted Neale, David Stech, Bud Koller, Regis Minerd, Kelly Grudzinski, John Higgs and a few others. They are not only my colleagues, they are my good friends. I am fortunate to have a number of good friends like them. They visited me often while I was in the hospital. They were all genuinely concerned for me, and they stuck with me throughout the entire episode.

I believe it was also the same day when my blood sugar went too low due to improper mixes of the insulin in my intra-venous system. My daughter and my wife were present at the time. I was having a conversation with them. All of a sudden I started to say things such as, "Let's go home! This is not our home! What are we doing here, etc, etc?"

Soon, I went into a convulsion. Fortunately, the RN was readily available to give me a glucose shot, and quickly thereafter I came to my senses again.

Dr. P. V. also came to visit me before the evening was over. He also said that the situation would need to get further stabilized prior to having a surgery. "You are doing well. Keep it up!" said the doctor to me prior to leaving the room.

Next morning, Thursday, October 26, my wife came early in the morning, as I was scheduled to have a number of tests done.

One of them was a nuclear test. That test did not go well. First of all, there was a delay to start and, when I was taken down there, I had to lie down in a stationary position for more than an hour and a half underneath the special x-ray machine, I was not allowed to move at all. It was very difficult for me to stay in the same position for that length of time.

When the test was over, the technician told me, "You need to come back, and we will need to do it all over again."

I asked him for the reason and he said, "The machine was not working."

I was extremely disappointed and asked him for what purpose I had been lying in the same position for that long and why did they not discontinue the test earlier. I was so disappointed that I said to him, "I do not want to go through the same ordeal again."

They took me back to my room. I was very upset. My wife asked me to calm down. But I remained upset for sometime. A few hours later, the technicians called me again for the same test, and I said that I did not want to go through the same ordeal again. It was nothing but a torture, as well as punishment, for me, and it did not show any result.

As usual, Dr. E. S., Dr. M. D. and Dr. P. C. came to see my progress. Both Dr. M. D. and Dr. P. C. indicated that my condition was getting better and if the progress continued, I might be scheduled for my gall bladder surgery for Saturday, October 28.

Both of them asked me to get myself mentally prepared for the operation. Dr. M. D. commented on my progress stating that it was amazing how my condition was improving especially when I was not having any direct medication to remedy the root causes.

Later that day Dr. U. K. also visited me. He looked through all of my charts and reports.

He said to me, "It is a miraculous improvement! You are doing really well. With this kind of progress undoubtedly we can proceed with the gall bladder operation."

He stayed in the room for a few minutes longer, and he told me that he had been associated with this hospital for the past forty-two years. With the complication I had, he found my amazing recovery to be a miraculous situation. He also asked me to keep it up and be mentally prepared for the upcoming surgery.

I was ready to tell Dr. U. K. what actually transpired outside this world as I met God at the Gateway to the Kingdom of Heaven when God said to me, "I am sending you back to the earth. Go back until I see you again next time." But then I thought that it might not be the appropriate moment to disclose this truth to a senior medical professional. Therefore, I remained silent for the time being. My wife thanked Dr. U. K. for his visit, and he said that he would see me again prior to the scheduled date of operation.

When the visiting hours were over that evening my wife and my daughter left for home. I kept thinking, "What actually did take place last Saturday?" I became curious to find out. I decided to ask Dr. M. D., as well as my wife when I see them again next time.

Next morning was Friday, October 27. Dr. E. S. was always the very first doctor who came to see me. As usual, Dr. M. D. also came to see me. I was going to ask him for the details about the previous Saturday, but before I could, he said to me, "Listen! I need to tell you something. I will not be able to come and see you for the next seven days. I'll be away."

I asked him where he was going. He said, "I will be going to San Francisco to attend a medical seminar."

He continued to say, "Don't worry! I arranged for another doctor. His name is Dr. M. L. and he will look after you on my behalf while I am gone."

"Dr. M. L. is a good doctor and I've known him for quite some time. You will be in good hands. Dr. M. L. will also keep me informed of your progress. You be good. I want to see you in good shape after I return," he checked my reports and left.

After Dr. M. D. left, I was a little sad for two reasons: first, I did not expect him to leave until I got better (but then I understood that attending his professional seminars is also important) and second, I did not have a chance to ask him about last Saturday. He seemed to be in a hurry that day. Most likely he had to take care of his last-minute tasks prior to his journey.

I must admit that all of the Registered Nurses and Health Care professionals who took care of me were excellent. They always treated me with utmost care and love. Each person was incredible. I cannot remember all of their names now, but all of them deserve my appreciation, as without their dedication, I could not have gotten better so quickly.

As I was waiting for my wife to arrive that day, the nurse on duty entered the room and monitored the machine. When she finished her task, I asked her, "May I ask you a question?"

She replied, "Certainly."

I said to her, "I really would like to speak to the nurse who attended me last Tuesday when I opened my eyes. Could you kindly find out who that person was and ask her to see me?" She said, "Certainly! I will find out who was on duty that day and let you know." She went away from the room.

A little later, she returned to my room with a young lady. She said to me, "She is the one who was on duty last Tuesday." I looked at her and said, "Sorry! The lady who was here with me was much older." I described how she looked. They said, "Nobody works here by that description." I did not know what to say in response. I stopped asking. But I still remember the face of that motherly-type nurse.

Recollection Of Events

Soon my wife came to see me. After a short conversation, I asked her, "So tell me what exactly happened last Saturday? I would like to know."

She said that after the Emergency Response Team failed to bring me to life in the Intensive Care Unit, some of the doctors decided to send me to the Critical Care Unit so that I could receive a twenty-four hour/around-the-clock care.

I asked, "Why would they send me to the CCU if they could not revive me at ICU?"

She said, "Your breathing stopped and your heart beat stopped. There were no signs of your vital life, but somehow some of the doctors determined that your brain was still functioning. That's the reason they brought you to CCU. They put you on artificial life support immediately. A lot of doctors and nurses had been working on you continuously."

After they moved you to CCU, they stopped everyone from visiting you, including me.

I asked my wife, "What did you do then?"

She said, "Our son, daughter-in-law and our granddaughter, we were asked to wait in the lounge area. We were not allowed to come and see you. I did not know what to do. I was totally at a loss."

She said, "I asked our son to call Frank, Joe and Regis."

Frank is the General Manager of the company I work for. Frank and I have been working for the same company for many years. The relationship is not limited to employer and employee, but also as family and friends. Joe and I have been colleagues for many years. We have been friends for a long period of time. Regis had been my immediate boss for a number of years. Outside of work, our relationship was more like friends, with mutual respect.

She continued, "Frank and his wife, Ann, came very promptly. Soon Regis and his wife, Marilyn, came. Joe came a little later as he had difficulty finding the hospital."

We all sat down and discussed your situation. They were all shocked to hear the update. At one point, Dr. M. D. joined us. He hugged me and said, "His condition is very critical. I am sorry." Dr. M. D. was upset over the whole situation.

She continued, "Dr. U. K. also joined us, and we were all talking about your condition."

She continued, "I said to Dr. M. D., I went to see him, but they would not let me in." They said, 'Only the physicians are allowed.' Dr. M. D. said, "Do you want to see him? Come with me.'"

My wife continued, "I went to see you, along with Dr. M. D. Your condition was very critical. It appeared to me that you had left us forever. I could not stay in that room for long. I came out."

Dr. M. D. said, 'Only one person at a time can go and see him.'

I said, 'Let Frank go first.' Frank came and saw you. He was emotionally distressed after he saw you. Dr. M. D. also allowed our son and daughter-in-law to see you. They all became emotional and did not know what to say. They could not imagine that the situation would turn so critical so suddenly."

I asked, "Do we know what caused me to collapse last Saturday?"

She said, "You remember when the doctor was draining the fluid out of your lung, and I told you I did not see much fluid, but blood. One of your arteries inside the lung got pierced, and it was continuously bleeding inside the lung. Gradually, your lung got filled with blood, your breathing stopped, you collapsed, and your heart stopped. The emergency response team tried their best to revive you, and they were not having much success."

I asked, "What happened after that?"

She continued, "I think the doctors took you to the surgery room. You were there for quite some time. Dr. J. L., who is the top-notch surgeon in this hospital, installed several drain tubes into the left side of your chest and drained the blood out. You were also continuously given blood transfusion, since you had already lost most of your own blood."

She said, "Then it was getting late at night. One by one, they all left, and we also went home."

She continued, "On our journey back home I said to our son and daughter-in-law not to say anything about your collapse and the critical situation to our daughter. Up until then, she was completely in the dark of your situation. She will not be able to handle this news emotionally. I told them, 'We will gradually disclose the situation.'"

They nodded.

I asked her, "Does she know by now what happened to me?"

"Not quite," she said, "She knows only bits and pieces. You are going through a series of tests, and you will be in the hospital for some time."

Soon it was late afternoon of that day. I told my wife to go to the cafeteria downstairs and have something to eat. She was always on the go; she was not taking care of herself; she was not having her meals routinely; she had no time for her own. Reluctantly, she went downstairs to the cafeteria.

Bud Koller, a good friend of mine came to see me. We spoke for a while, and, when my wife returned to the room, Bud stayed for a few minutes longer and then he left. No other doctor visited me that day. I was still waiting for a confirmation as to whether or not I was going to have the surgery the next day.

Next morning, Saturday, October 28, Dr. M. L. came to see me. I asked him if I was going to have the surgery that day. He said that he was not sure, and it was all up to Dr. P. C., the surgeon.

Later, Dr. P. C. came to see me and advised that he decided to postpone my operation until Monday, October 30. He continued, "During the weekend, the doctors usually take care of the emergencies only." He said that it would work better for him, as well as for me, if he scheduled it for Monday. I agreed.

During that weekend, I had a number of visitors - colleagues from my workplace, as well as family and friends. Dr. U. K. also came to see me on both Saturday and Sunday. He stayed for a little longer than normal and tried to cheer me up. He said that my condition was getting stabilized for the operation. He said, "It is better that the operation got postponed until Monday. By Monday, your condition would get a little more stabilized." He also commented that it was a miraculous improvement. He wished me well for my surgery on Monday and left.

Gangrenous Gall Bladder

On Monday, October 30, my wife came to see me early. In the morning, I was going through the pre-surgery procedures. I was not concerned. I knew that God would not have sent me back to the earth with some specific instructions for me to follow if He had to call me back to Him so soon. I knew that I would be fine.

I was mentally prepared for the operation. I think my wife was concerned. Of course, she had all the reasons to be concerned. Considering all the circumstances I was going through since October 18 and the fact that she was with me at each step of the way, that experience alone would be sufficient reason for her to be worried.

She asked me, "You are still weak. What do you think? Will you be ok to go through this? I am worried for you." I said to her, "Don't worry! I'm prepared to go through this. Let's get it done! I will be ok."

Soon they took me to the operating room. Once I was there I was given the anesthesia, and within a few seconds I fell into deep sleep. Later, when I was recovering from the anesthesia, I saw Dr. P. C. was standing beside me and talking to me. He was saying, "Everything went fine. We will keep you for a few minutes longer under observation before we can send you back to your room."

I asked if my wife was anywhere nearby. The doctor said that they would call her, and she would be allowed to come in.

My wife soon came by me. She said, "Thank God! Everything went smoothly."

I asked her how long it took. I believe she said it was about two to three hours since I came in. She held my hand and said, "I was waiting at the lounge. The doctor came to see me after the operation and sat beside me. The doctor said that he removed the gall bladder. He also removed the stones. He took more time than normal as he was carefully probing the surrounding areas. He said that everything went fine. They would also do some biopsy on the removed gall bladder for further analysis."

My wife kept me good company, while the nurses were keeping an eye on me every few minutes. They were continuously monitoring my vitals, and, when they were convinced that I was ok to go back to my room, they sent me there.

The nurses on my floor were excited to see me back and were anxious to make me feel comfortable. They quickly transferred me to my bed and adjusted the position. I was still under the influence of anesthesia and my mind was still foggy.

I believe Dr. M. L. came to see me twice that day, once prior to the surgery and again after the surgery. I remember I also had a few floor physicians who came to see me, and they were looking at my charts and checking the results of my operation.

By that evening the test results of my removed gall bladder was in my room. I remember one member of the medical team showing me my gall bladder and some stones that were removed from my body. They were kept inside a plastic or glass container. I was also advised that the removed gall bladder was "gangrenous". My wife asked, "What does that mean?"

The person said, "In plain English, he has been very lucky. If the gall bladder was not removed from his body at this time, the gangrene set in his gall bladder would remove him from this world. Gangrenes are very nasty and deadly."

When the medical person left the room, my wife said, "Thank God! The gangrenous gall bladder was removed right in time. Otherwise, it would have been too late."

Later, when the nurse was changing the dressings from the incision areas, I noticed that a tube was protruding from the right side of my stomach into a bulb-shaped container. I asked the nurse what that was for. She said it was meant for drainage of the excess bile. It had to be frequently monitored. Whenever it was near full, it needed to be drained, measured and recorded each time. She also said, "It will stay there for several days until the surgeon removes it from your body."

In the evening, my daughter came to see me, and my wife returned home with her after the regular visiting hours were over.

I could not sleep that night, since I felt that I was taken over by different kinds of pain. The pain from the wounds of incisions had taken over my whole body. At times, it was intolerable and prevented me from falling asleep. For the first time in my life, I asked the attending RN for some pain killers. I never liked taking any pain killers and always avoided them.

I was then given pain killers, but I noticed the effect was not long lasting and very temporary. At the same time, I was having nightmares or some weird dreams, such as I was forcefully kept in a house. I wanted to escape from there but had no way of getting out, since the people who forcefully kept me there were watching me all the time. As long as the pain killers were in effect, I was not feeling the pain as my mind was occupied with having the same weird dream over and over. It was a very strange feeling, and I never enjoyed these dreams.

The night passed somehow, and then it was Tuesday, October 31. As usual, Dr. E. S. came to see me in the morning. A little later, Dr. M. L. also came. Nothing much happened that day. I was trying to recover from the pains of the surgery.

Mini Surgery & Oxygen Therapy

Later that evening, I noticed that I was experiencing difficulty breathing again. My wife stayed with me practically the whole day and went home after the regular visiting hours were over.

I fell asleep. Sometime late in the night, I was awakened by the resident nurse and the doctor. They were very concerned by an earlier x-ray that showed that I was having some fresh blood in my lungs which was not getting drained out. They said that I needed another drain tube put in my lungs immediately, or things might get complicated.

The resident doctor, the registered nurse and a patient care assistant prepared themselves for a mini-surgery right there in my bed. The doctor applied the local anesthesia and performed the mini-surgery and implanted another drain tube from my left lung. I was not put to sleep. Therefore, I was able to look at the entire operation.

After the medical team left the room, I began to wonder if the operation was carried out properly and whether or not it should have been done in the proper surgery room by a more experienced surgical team. I said to myself, "There must be something wrong inside, and they could not wait that long."

I decided to ask my doctor about this when I saw him the next time. But Dr. M. D., my family physician, still had not returned from his San Francisco trip.

The next day, November 1, when Dr. M. L. came to visit me, I told him what actually happened the night before. I asked him whether the mini-surgery conducted in the room was a routine procedure. I also asked him, "If my condition had gotten worse and if there were complications, how would that be handled?"

Dr. M. L. was surprised to hear that such an operation took place without the consent of the patient or a close family member. He said, "Normally, the hospital should have contacted your spouse or a nearest family member advising of the situation." He did not know why it was not done.

My wife came to see me later, and I told her about the previous night. She was completely in the dark up to that point not knowing that such an action had taken place, and she was completely unaware of it. She wanted to ask the hospital administrator for an explanation. I told her not to pursue the matter any further, as this could complicate the medical treatment.

She said that a lot of things happened in the last two weeks, and she was not objecting to the unscheduled operation being done in the room. She said, "At least they could have advised me what they were going to do, and I could have been present at the time."

I said to her not to worry about it, since everything went fine.

But everything was not fine. My problem with breathing started to get worse. Soon, I was put back on the oxygen tube. Also, I was placed on the breathing therapy several times a day.

Soon the night fell, and visiting hours were over. My wife insisted that she was not going back home. She would rather stay there with me throughout the night. At least she would be able to keep an eye on me. I said to her, "There are nurses and other health care professionals who are here, and it is their job to take care of me. Perhaps, they won't allow you to stay."

She went out and came back a few minutes later. She said, "I asked the RN, and there was no problem for me to stay here overnight."

She pointed to a chair in the room and said, "This chair can fold into a bed, and I can sleep here. They will provide me with the pillows and cover sheets."

Even though I was concerned for the lack of her comfort, I noticed that she was quite pleased with the arrangement, and she looked happy. I was also happy to see her staying in the room, as I could have a companion and someone to talk to during the night should there be a need.

The night progressed. I asked her a few times if she was comfortable lying there, and she said she was fine.

As the night progressed, I was having more difficulty in breathing and I was in terrible discomfort. We take a lot of things for granted when we are healthy - breathing is one of them. It is one of the very basic needs for our survival. I'd have never realized how important the breathing was until I was in terrible discomfort.

I was immediately put on oxygen therapy. The RN kept increasing the percentage of oxygen, and, at one point, she raised the percentage of oxygen to 100%. I was always under the impression that 100% oxygen would be the purest and the most desirable form of air that we would like to breathe. When she said that I had to have one hundred percent oxygen therapy for the next four to six hours, I thought, "Great! I am going to have pure oxygen to inhale for that long period of time. It is cool."

But I was totally wrong about my thought. This therapy was so uncomfortable, and it definitely felt like a torture. Sometimes, when I could not tolerate it any more, I was disconnecting the attachment from my nose and mouth. The RN was observing me all the time, and every time I was disconnecting it for a few seconds she would get angry at me. She said that if I did one more time she would put my hands in a restraint.

Occasionally, I could not tolerate it any more and cried out loudly several times, begging her to stop this therapy. But the therapy did not stop. It continued through the entire night into the next morning.

Now it was Thursday, November 2. The ratio of oxygen was gradually reduced much lower. I said to myself, "What a relief! Finally, the torture has stopped."

Major Lung Surgery

As usual, Dr. E. S. came to see me in the morning. She asked me typically the same questions. Dr. M. L. also came to see me, along with Dr. U. K. The doctors advised that I would have to go through several x-rays that day and the next morning. Depending on the results of the x-rays, a decision would be made as to whether or not I would need a surgery in my lungs. Accordingly, I was scheduled to have several x-rays that day.

When the results of the x-rays were received, I was advised by the resident doctor that a surgery was necessary. I was advised that it would be scheduled for Friday, November 3. I was also advised that this would be considered a major surgery, since it would take many hours in the operating room.

My wife asked the doctor, "Do you think he is medically fit to go through such a long procedure?"

The doctor said. "We have no alternatives. This surgery is absolutely necessary for his well-being. If we do not proceed with this, the consequences will not be good."

The doctor continued, "On the brighter side, let me tell you, you are fortunate that the surgery will be performed by Dr. J. L. who is associated with a world class hospital and considered to be one of the best doctors. He is well regarded as one of the top-notch surgeons."

The doctor continued, "We would put you on pre-surgical procedures tonight, and you would not be allowed to have any food or drinks for x number of hours. In the morning, you will need to have a few more x-rays prior to going to the operating room." The doctor then left the room.

My wife appeared to be nervous. She wanted me to get better, but she was not sure if physically I would be able to withstand such a major operation. She said to me, "You just went through a surgery last Monday. Today is Thursday. Not even four days have gone by. Now, they are talking about another major operation tomorrow that is supposed to last many hours. How would you handle this one? You have not yet recovered from the last one. You are still having aches and pains from the last incisions." I saw her mental stress and agony and realized what she was going through.

I said to my wife, "Don't worry. Everything will be fine. Dr. J. L. is the same doctor who put my drain tubes in the first place. I still have the tubes hanging on the left side of my chest. Dr. J. L. is a good surgeon. He came to see me several times and looks like a very caring type. I have full confidence in him. Nothing will happen to me."

She was still not feeling at ease with the situation. I insisted that she go home that night, since she needed a good night's sleep. The previous night, she was awake the whole night because of my 100% oxygen therapy. She saw throughout the entire night how uncomfortable I felt with that therapy.

I also suggested that she call our son and ask him to be present during the surgery. He lives in the state of Michigan. If he could stay with her throughout the operation and until the result was known, that definitely would provide moral support for her. In the event the situation became a crisis, his presence with his Mother would be very beneficial.

My wife went back home in the evening. She called my son and asked him if it was possible for him to take the time off work and be present at the hospital during the operation. My son said that he would be there. He did not know exactly when, but sometime during the day he would be there.

All along I was being nurtured through the inter-venous system. It was disconnected sometime in the evening, since I was expected to undergo the surgery in the morning. The RN came in quite frequently throughout the night to monitor and record various readings for charts that might be necessary for the surgeon to make his final decision.

I knew it would be a major surgery, but I did not feel nervous. I was rather anxious to have it over and done with. I was probably given a few tranquilizers earlier in the evening since I slept fairly well that night, despite my breathing problems and other pains.

Soon it was Friday, November 3. Dr. E. S. came to see me as usual. The technicians came twice to take x-rays. My wife came early in the morning knowing that I would be taken for the operation sometime in the morning, since she wanted to be there.

Sometime in the mid-morning I was taken to the surgery room. Dr. J. L. explained the procedure to me and introduced me to another surgeon who was going to assist him. I believe his name was Dr. J. S. There were a few other doctors and nurses who were discussing the case among themselves. I could gather from the discussions that I would be put on the artificial life support machine again.

My wife was asked to wait in the lounge, since the doctors may want to consult with her from time to time. She wished me "good luck" and went to the lounge.

I believe it was Dr. J. S. who gave me the anesthetics. Immediately, I fell into deep sleep. I had no idea what happened to me or where I was.

It felt very uncomfortable as I was coming off the anesthesia. A few doctors and nurses were talking to me, but I did not understand what they were saying. It felt strange because I was breathing through the artificial life support again.

It was so uncomfortable, and I was wishing to go back to sleep again. It felt like something strange had been stuck to my throat, and I could not move or get rid off it. I was dozing on and off again. I had absolutely no clue where I was or what I was doing at the time.

I remember seeing my wife once beside me, and then I was sleepy again. I was also feeling very weak. There were two nurses by my side, and they were saying something to me, but I did not understand one word.

I do not know how long I was in the recovery room. I do remember one doctor coming to me and saying, "You have been very brave. Everything is fine." At one point, I was thinking, "Why is it night-time already? I remember I came here in the morning. Why is it so dark already? It feels like it is quite late in the night."

I remember bits and pieces of my recovery. Once when I opened my eyes, I saw I was getting a blood transfusion. Another time I saw my hands and legs were restrained again like the previous time. I remember a doctor or a technician continuously monitoring the artificial breathing machine.

I do not know exactly when I came back to my full senses after the operation. It could very well have been the following morning, Saturday, November 4.

I remember seeing Dr. M. L., who told me that it was a very long operation, and I had lost a lot of blood. Consequently, they had to replenish the blood. He also said that the blood level in my system was still dangerously low, and he was keeping an eye on it. Should the blood level continue to slide, he would put in a request for another transfusion.

Dr. M. L. also said that Dr. M. D., my family physician had returned from his trip, and he would visit me soon.

I saw my wife a few times after the operation. However, I was not able to have a direct communication, since I was not steady. When I saw her later, I asked her if she managed to get some sleep the night before, and she said, "I did."

I asked her, "How long was I in the operating room?"

She said, "You were there five to six hours. But, since you had problems coming off the anesthesia, it took much longer."

I asked her, "What did you do all this time? Didn't you get bored?"

She said, "I was waiting in the lounge area. At one point, Dr. P. V. saw me and sat beside me. We discussed your operation, and he gave me moral support."

"What about our son? Did he ever come and stay with you, and how long did he stay?" I asked.

She said, "He came late and stayed for awhile. He was continuously on his cell phone, and he had to leave early because he had some urgent business to take care of."

I asked, "Did he call you after he left?" She said, "Yes, and he would be back on Sunday."

She continued, "I was waiting in the lounge for a long period of time. It felt like time was at a standstill. I could not go anywhere, since I was afraid that, if I went somewhere, Dr. J. L. might come out and look for me. He would probably go back to the operating room without talking to me. I was getting tensed as hours went by, and the doctor did not come out of the operating room. I was wondering if everything was going alright in the surgery area.

"Then, finally, the doctor came out, shook my hand and sat beside me. He said that it was a very complex operation. He said that he took extra caution and made sure everything was done properly. He also said that he found some blood stains inside the lungs, and he ensured the stains were all removed. He said that, 'If the stains did not get removed, your husband would not be well for long. That is why it took such a long time.'

He paused for a moment and continued, 'Let us hope for the best. Your husband will most likely need extra care for some time, even after he recovers from all this.'

He again paused for a moment and continued, 'You can see him when he is in the recovery room. It will take awhile before he recovers completely. He will be on the respiratory machine for some time and will also be receiving blood, since he lost some of his own."

My wife said, "Thank you, Dr. L.! Thank you so much for your extra care and dedication. We really appreciate it."

The doctor said, "You are welcome! You may come with me if you wish to peek at him. He must be in the recovery room."

My wife followed.

"What happened after that?" I asked.

She said, "You were still in a deep sleep and breathing through the respiratory machine again like last time. A couple of nurses were observing you. They said, 'It may take another half an hour to an hour. You may go some place and come back again.'"

My wife said, "I went to the cafeteria downstairs, had a cup of tea and light snack. I returned to the recovery room, and you were still not awake. The nurses said, 'He is taking his time. You may go out for another round and come back.'

"Gradually, all of the other patients who had surgeries earlier recovered and returned to their rooms. You were the only one remaining there. A few nurses and a small medical team were waiting for you to wake up so they could send you back to your room before they could call it a day.

"When you were finally brought to your room, a medical team was continuously working with the breathing machine for a long period of time. Your hands and feet were restrained one more time. The medical team said that they would remain with you until the respiratory machine was replaced by a normal oxygen tube."

My wife said, "I returned home after the normal visiting hours were over, since you needed a complete rest from the long surgery."

Amazing Bounce Back To Life

Next day, Saturday, November 4, Dr. M. D., my family physician came to see me, and I was delighted to see him back. The last time I saw him was a week earlier on Friday, October 27.

I suppose that Dr. M. D. was also anxious to see me, since he said that he came straight from the airport. He was on his way home and decided to stop by and see how I was doing.

He asked me how I was feeling. I said, "Much better than last time when you saw me."

He looked at my charts and said, "It is a miracle. I'm really impressed. Your condition is much better. If you keep it up, you will be able to go home soon."

This is the first time I heard any doctor speaking to me about the possibility of going home. I can now feel the joy of hope. Just a mere thought of going home cheered me up. Was I really seeing the light at the end of tunnel? I asked myself.

Dr. M. D. left the room to speak to the resident staff and came back a few minutes later.

"Just hang in there, and I will see you tomorrow. Keep it up. You are doing great," he said to me before he left.

I asked my wife if she wanted to go home and take some rest. She said, "I can take some rest here on this chair." I agreed.

As far as I can recall, she had stayed in the room for several nights. She always kept an eye on me and made sure that I was not feeling depressed. Sometimes I was getting concerned for her not getting enough sleep, but she was happy to be there with me.

The night passed, and then it was Sunday, November 5. Both Dr. M. D. and Dr. M. L. came to see me and they were pleased with the progress I was making.

Shortly before noon my son, my daughter-in-law and my granddaughter came to see me. My wife and I were both very happy to see them. I told them that their mother needed to get out of this room. I told them that I was doing much better, and it was time to celebrate. I asked them to go to a good restaurant and enjoy a good lunch. They complied.

After a few hours, they came back. We chatted for awhile, and they departed shortly thereafter. My wife left with them also, since they indicated they would drop her home.

After they left, later that evening, my blood sugar dropped too low again due to a high amount of insulin in the system. It dropped so low that I went into a convulsion, and luckily there was a doctor nearby. The nurse told me the next day that the doctor gave me a glucose shot, and soon I was back to my senses.

When my wife found out about the incident the next day (Monday, November 6), that I was on convulsion again for the second time, she was not too pleased. She said to me, "For the next few days, until you get released from this hospital, I am staying here in this room day and night. I cannot afford to lose you again." I said to her, "Nobody did it on purpose. Mistakes do happen. That's why we are humans."

"They should be more careful, as it is a matter of life and death," she said. Later, when the nurse came to my room, the nurse apologized to me for what happened the previous night. She said that it was an honest mistake, and she felt very sorry for the incident. My wife calmed down, and we all were friends again.

A number of doctors visited me on Monday, November 6. They were Dr. E. S., Dr. G. H., Dr. J. S., Dr. M. D., Dr. P. V., Dr. J. L., and Dr. R. F.

Everyone congratulated me on my impressive recovery. A few of them commented to me that it was undoubtedly a miraculous, hard to believe type of recovery.

Dr. J. L. said to me, "As soon as the drain pipes come off your chest, you would be able to go home."

I asked Dr. J. L., "When do you think they will come off?" He said, "Within a few days. I have to ask them to take x-rays of your chest daily. I will take them off as soon as the x-rays indicate that they could come off."

Dr. J. L. also suggested for me to start walking a couple of times each day. "You will need to gain your strength back before we can release you from the hospital."

Dr. R. F. came to me and said, "Good Luck and Best Wishes to you. You do not need me any more. Therefore, I will not see you again."

He said to me that he enjoyed working with my case. He wished me well and shook my hands before he left. Both my wife and I thanked him for his dedication and care.

Unexpected Apology From Dr. X

Around the same time, both my wife and I noticed that Dr. X, who did the surgery at my back on Saturday, October 21, had been coming by my room quite frequently as if he wanted to say something to me.

Every time he came by my room, both my wife and I were not happy to see him at all. As a matter of fact, whenever he came by us, we were feeling tensed up. When my family physician, Dr. M. D. came to see me, we requested him to tell Dr. X that he needs to stay away from this room. We really did not want to see him again.

However, one day shortly thereafter, Dr. X came to my room, and my wife was there in the room at that time.

He told me, "Listen, I know you do not want to see me, and I do not blame you for that. But I have to say something to you. Please grant me a couple of minutes. I know you get disturbed to see me. Please let me say what I need to say, and then I will not disturb you again."

I looked at my wife, and she looked at me. I said, "Ok, go ahead, you may continue."

The doctor said, "I have been trying to come and speak to you several times in the past few weeks. All my attempts have failed thus far. Every time I came to speak to you either you had someone in the room or you were not in a position to talk. I know you have told your doctor that you do not wish to see me near your room. But I need to tell you something so that I can get it off my chest."

I asked, "What do you want tell me?"

The doctor said, "I have come to ask for your forgiveness. Because of me, you have suffered a lot. I am so sorry. I have caused you a great deal of suffering and pain. Please forgive me. Unless you forgive me, I will not be able to rest in peace."

My wife and I looked at each other. While we were trying to decide how to respond to this unexpected situation, the doctor continued to say, "I have been practicing here for the past twelve or thirteen years. Anything like this has never happened before."

I remained quiet for a moment. The doctor continued, "Ever since that day I was not able to sleep at night. It keeps bothering me, and I cannot forgive myself. I stay awake most of the time at night, looking at the ceiling of my bedroom."

He continued to say, "I guess it proves that we are all human beings. Just because we are doctors does not mean that we do not make mistakes. I just want you to know that I did not do it on purpose. It was not intentional. I just feel so sorry, and I apologize to you. Please forgive me if you can."

I looked at my wife to watch her reaction whether or not I should accept his apology. She nodded.

I said to the doctor, "Doctor X, you have realized that you have made a mistake, and you said that you have not done this intentionally. Even though you are a doctor, you are still a human being, and all humans make mistakes. I am not keeping any grudges against you. You can rest in peace."

The doctor was touched by my comments. He shook my hand,

and wished me well and a speedy recovery. He also thanked us for our forgiveness and said that he felt much lighter, as if a big burden had been removed from his chest.

After the doctor left the room, I started to think, "This doctor is obviously very much disturbed by the circumstances that caused the situation to go totally out of control, and his conscience must be bothering him so much that he had been persistently trying to speak to me for several days."

However, I started to wonder, "Was the crisis really caused by this doctor? Or was there an Invisible Force Who had been working mysteriously behind the scenes to draw our attention?"

There is no doubt in my mind that an Invisible Force was totally responsible for the entire episode. I am thoroughly convinced that The Invisible Force was orchestrating the whole thing. What would be the purpose? That is still a mystery and far beyond our comprehension. How can we understand what goes through the logic of Infinity with our finite mind? We simply cannot.

Conversation With God

Let me go back to the Gateway of the Kingdom of Heaven and refresh how I met God and how the conversations went.

Back on the altar at the Gateway, as I was looking towards the center of the high walled platform, my eyes were struck in awe at what I saw. At the center of that location was a huge throne. Lo and behold! There was the Lord! The Lord was sitting on the throne!

As soon as I saw Him, I knew He was the Supreme Lord! I started to tremble with fear! He was so huge. Here, I am 5'6" tall, standing at the extreme far left corner and looking at the center of that altar, and He is approximately 600 feet away from me. He was sitting on the throne, and, at that sitting position, He appeared to be approximately 35 to 40 feet tall. Therefore, when He stands up, I presume He would be about 70 feet tall. He was very well proportioned and wore a white robe.

I again started to tremble with fear, and my knees felt very weak. I was standing at the extreme far edge of the platform, and I could very easily fall off the edge with my fearful trembling. He was such a powerful, overwhelming and mesmerizing figure that I could not look at Him for too long. I was trembling with fear so much thinking that this would be the end of my life. The Lord will not spare me.

I looked slightly towards the left of the throne (right from my position) and was amazed to see a very narrow door. The door was so narrow that it struck me as completely out of proportion. I now realized that this narrow door is the only entrance to the inside of the Kingdom of Heaven. This is the only entrance in the entire perimeter of the compound. This is the entrance for which I had been searching.

"How do I go through this door?" I asked myself. The Lord is so big and frightening I cannot dare myself to go near the door. It was quite evident to me that I could not even try to enter through the door, unless the Lord allowed me to go through the door.

It had been also pretty clear to me that I was now standing at the Gateway to the Kingdom of Heaven, and I was completely at the mercy of the Lord. I was still nervous and shaky, but then the Lord spoke to me.

He had a very deep, commanding voice, but, at the same time, I noticed His voice was also a loving one. Language did not seem to be a barrier at all. When the Lord spoke, I could understand that in any of the languages I know. By the same token, it didn't matter in what language I responded - the Lord understood every word, even before I spoke.

The Lord looked at me and asked, "What are you doing here?"

I shrugged my shoulders, meaning, "I do not know."

He said to me in an authoritative, but loving voice, "Your time has not come yet. I'm sending you back to the earth. Go back until your time comes."

By then, I gathered some courage, as I noticed I was not shaking any longer with fear. The Lord continued, "Go back and complete your unfinished tasks. Love your family. Love your children. Pay attention to your daughter – she needs your help."

Hearing the loving and caring voice of the Lord, I gathered a little more courage, and I asked, "Lord! I'm not worthy of standing before

You. I'm a sinner! I have sinned, Lord. How can I be sure that I can enter through this door next time? Lord, please tell me - when is my next time?"

The Lord did not respond.

I continued to plead, "Lord! Please provide me with some guidance. How can I prepare myself for the next time? How can I make myself worthy of standing before you next time? I do not know how much time I'll have before the next time."

The Lord still did not respond.

I continued pleading, "Please Lord! Please guide me to prepare myself for next time. Please tell me if I need to join any church, any temple, any synagogue, any religious institute, any religious association or any other place. I'll do whatever You say, but please guide me."

The Lord looked at me and said, "No, it is not necessary for you to join any church, any temple or anything else. Those things are not important to Me."

(Although the Lord indicated to me that membership to any religious group is not necessary to enter the Kingdom of Heaven, we, as humans, definitely need a support group to help us through our difficult times, remind us of the importance of worshiping God, teach us in the Ways of the Lord, and assist us in accomplishing His directives.)

The Lord continued, "What is important to Me is your personal relationship with Me, how sincere, how honest, how true are you with Me? That's the only thing that counts."

I looked at the Lord and begged Him to be merciful to me.

I said, "Lord! I am a human being. When I go back, I'll be involved with my day-to-day activities, and I'll be back to my worldly life. Please give me some specific instructions or guidelines that I can follow." I continued to beg for His mercy.

Specific Instructions From God

The Lord looked at me and said, "Here are some instructions for you that I want you to follow between now and your next time."

He gave me the following five instructions.

1. "TELL THE TRUTH"

"Go back and tell the truth. Do not be afraid to tell the truth. Some people may ridicule upon you when they hear the truth, but do not despair, be brave and always tell the truth."

('Truth' here for me has dual meanings. Tell the truth in the sense has meaning 'do not lie'. But, in the broader sense, He is asking me to tell about my experience at the Gateway to the Kingdom of Heaven, my meeting Him in person, my discovery of the one and only narrow entry door to Heaven, His kind conversations with me, His specific instructions to me, and so on. By His first instruction to me He is not only asking me not to lie, but also He is asking me to go back and share my experience with everyone without any fear.)

2. "COMMIT NO MORE SINS"

"From this day on forward, do not commit any more sins. Remember the consequences. The wages of sin is death."

(All my sins up to that day had been forgiven by Him as He is asking me "From this day on forward do not commit any more sins." However, "Sin" in the eyes of God may not exactly be the same as we humans view it. We are all committing sins every day knowingly or unknowingly. I try my best not to commit any more sins every day. But our day-to-day life style in this world is such that I cannot say for sure that I am not committing any more sins. What I view as not sin may very well be sinful in the eyes of God.)

3. "SURRENDER YOURSELF COMPLETELY TO ME IN YOUR DAILY LIFE"

(By this instruction, He is asking me to surrender myself completely to Him. He is asking me to let Him be in the driver's seat. He is asking me to let Him take control over everything that is necessary for me to live through this life. Surrendering myself completely to Him means that He is taking charge of my life, and He will see that all my needs are fulfilled, since He knows what my needs are.)

4. "WALK WITH ME"

(I should have asked God what He specifically meant for me by this instruction. I am still not sure how I can walk with God. I am a human being. How can a human being walk with God? I have asked some of my friends and some spiritual leaders for their interpretations of this instruction. They have been kind enough to provide me with their best explanations, i.e., perhaps it means do not go ahead of me nor fall behind me; hold my hand and walk "with" me. But I am still searching for the true meaning of this instruction. I am hoping that through my prayers and meditation God will offer His guidance.)

5. "TAKE CARE OF THE POOR"

"Take care of the poor. Open your hearts. Be generous to the poor. They need your help."

Then, He repeated for the second time,

"TAKE CARE OF THE POOR. OPEN YOUR HEARTS. BE GENEROUS TO THEM. THEY NEED YOUR HELP. THIS IS VERY IMPORTANT."

(The word 'Poor' does not mean someone who needs financial help only; it can also mean someone who is physically, mentally, intellectually or spiritually poor and needing help.)

When the Lord repeated for the second time asking me to take care of the poor, stressing that this is very important and I need to be generous to the poor as they need my help and this is a very important instruction.

I said very humbly to the Lord, "Lord! Certainly I will help the poor as much as I can. You know the needs for the poor in the world are far greater than what a small person like me can do. The needs are not only where I live; the needs are everywhere, all over the world. "

"Lord! Please forgive me saying this. I will take care of the poor as much as I can, but my efforts will be like a tiny drop of water in the entire ocean. It is not going to make much of an impact."

As I said this to God, I was feeling extremely concerned that I should not have said anything like this to God. Definitely, He will be angry at me, and He will be very annoyed with me. I have no right to speak to Him like this. Who am I to tell God? He knows how big the needs are.

It is with great fear and great respect I said to the Lord, "Lord! Please forgive my sins. I should not have said anything like this to You. You are Almighty. You know everything. I did not mean to question your instruction. I am a simple human being. I am only trying to state that the needs to help the poor are far greater than what a small person like me can accomplish. Please forgive me. I beg for Your mercy!"

I was waiting for God to get angry at me and punish me for my rudeness. However, I was pleasantly surprised as I noticed that He was not annoyed with me at all. Instead, with a deep loving voice, He said to me, "Listen carefully! I am assigning you with a few tasks when you are back on the earth. I want you to complete your unfinished tasks. When you are back to the earth I want you to write two books."

He continued, "Go back and write the first book about telling the truth; about your experience; and about this conversation as it is taking place between you and Me. Do not be afraid to be truthful. I will ensure that this book reaches to the readers everywhere in the world."

The Lord looked at me and said, "For these tasks I am also giving you two guidelines for you to follow. You must remember them always. They are important."

"First, each and every penny that you will receive from the sales of the two books, you must give them away to the cause of the poor. You must not keep one penny from the proceeds for yourself. This is very important!"

"Second, you need to let your readers know that it is not important to Me at all whatever church, temple or religious institution they belong to. The most important one to Me is each person's own personal relationship with Me. I am only interested to know how sincere, how honest, how true they are with Me. Tell your readers that the five instructions that I am asking you to obey between now and your next time, the same instructions equally apply for every mankind. The fifth instruction is particularly important to each and every person. Everyone needs to open their hearts and be generous to the poor. I expect it from everyone."

I said to the Lord, "Thank You, Lord! Thank You for Your mercy! Lord, forgive me, I have never written a book in my life. But I will write as You are assigning the tasks to me. Please give me the strength and the courage so that I can complete my assignments. Lord, you said for me to write two books. When do you want me to write the second book?"

The Lord said, "Write the first one soon after you are back on your feet and then wait for a year or two before you start the next one. Do not be afraid. I will be with you and I will guide you."

By then, I noticed that I was not feeling afraid of God any more. To me, He was very kind, loving, and like a true friend with genuine concern for each and every one of us.

I asked God a few more questions. He answered all of them. It will not be appropriate for me to share the rest of the conversations with all my readers, since they are a bit personal and related to my family members. I sincerely apologize to my readers for not disclosing them.

When we finished our conversation, God said to me, "I am now sending you back to the earth. Go back and complete your unfinished tasks. When the time comes I will see you again."

I thanked the Lord for His mercy and love to me.

Next thing I remember is opening my eyes and seeing a loving, motherly type nurse looking at me in the hospital room. Who was that nurse?

I remember very clearly about my journey from the earth to the Gateway of the Kingdom of Heaven. I described that journey earlier in this book. I was following a very bright light at a tremendous speed for a considerable amount of time until I reached my destination on the other side.

But I do not remember anything at all how I returned from the

Gateway to the Kingdom of Heaven back to the earth. However, I know one thing for sure - this is a journey that I was not allowed to do on my own. A companion bright light had to take me there.

The question still remains - how did I get back from there to here? Considering this is a journey I cannot make on my own, someone had to bring me back from there to here.

Was the loving motherly type nurse whom I saw was none other than an Angel sent by God? Was it her assignment to return me to my destination back to the earth, safe and sound?

This will remain a mystery to me for the rest of my life.

Release From The Hospital

Meanwhile, back in the hospital, my progress was remarkably fast. All of the drain tubes came off my chest one by one. My IV tubes came off. For the first time in three weeks I was allowed to have solid food, namely, Jell-O. All of the tubes that were attached to my body came off one by one. I felt a great relief.

I was bed-ridden all this time. I started to walk again just like a child - first with the help of a trained nurse, then with my wife assisting me, a few times with my visiting friend, Bud, and another few times with an extraordinary Patient Care Assistant named Dan. Dan helped me very often whenever he was on duty.

I remember when Dan took me one afternoon for a short walk outside the door to fetch some fresh air for the first time since I got admitted into the hospital, he said to me, "Can you smell the Pine trees? Try to smell and take a deep breath of fresh air and hold it for a few seconds. Thank the Lord as you are holding it, because we take a lot of things for granted in our life. We do not appreciate the things until they are taken away from us."

Dan, I will never forget those words as long as I live. You are absolutely right. We do not know how to thank God for all the little things that He gave us to enjoy, such as the smell of a Pine tree and the natural air we breathe for us to survive in our daily life, we definitely take them for granted.

We do not appreciate the love and mercy of God for all the little things, not until they are taken away from us. It is absolutely true.

Finally, the day came. It was the day I was anxiously waiting for. Many times I seriously thought that I would never see this day again in my life.

It was Friday, November 10, 2006.

Dr. M. D., my family physician came to my room and announced that I would be released from the hospital that afternoon. However, he said that I would be put under a very close observation. A visiting Home Healthcare Nurse would visit me on a regular basis to observe and monitor my progress.

I was also scheduled to have follow-up visits to most of the doctors and surgeons who took care of me.

My wife accompanied me to all of those visits. Once she asked the doctor, "How can we be certain that his wounded pancreas is completely heeled? As far as we know, he did not receive any medications or treatments for it. How do we know that it won't resurface?"

The doctor said, "All the symptoms indicate that he does not currently have any major problem. But to ensure, I'm going to ask for an MRCP."

I asked the doctor, "What is an MRCP?"

The doctor said, "It is sort of an ultrasonic test called Magnetic Resonance Cholangiopancreatography. We will make an appointment for you. It needs to be done in the hospital lab. It is recommended that you fast for two to four hours before the test, and it will take approximately 30 minutes to complete the procedure."

Fearfully I asked, "Do I need to have anesthetics again?"

The doctor replied with a smile, "Not at all. It is a special kind of an x-ray. There is nothing to worry about."

Return To Regular Activities

Within a few weeks of my release from the hospital I completed all of my post-surgery check-ups and required tests. Everything was fine. Dr. M. D. initially released me for half-day at work for a couple of weeks and finally released me for full-day at work. Through the grace of God, I was back to my day-to-day activities in a short period of time.

From the time the trauma started up until the time I met God in person, everything was working against me. My condition at the ICU was getting more and more complicated with one thing after another going for me in the wrong direction. There was no medication; no treatment, not until my heart rate would come down; there was no help in sight. I felt all along that an Invisible Force was working behind the scenes to make His points known to me.

As soon as I met God and when He said to me, "I am sending you back to the earth until I see you again next time," I noticed my conditions started to turn positive with or without explanations.

God provided me with highly skilled surgeons and highly knowledgeable medical teams, in a highly caring environment. Without His help, how could I turn around from the extremely dangerous heart rate condition to go through an extended gall bladder operation within a few days? How was it possible that the gangrenous gall bladder was removed just in time? How was it possible that the gangrenes did not remove me from this world before they were removed? How did I get better from the viral pneumonia? How could I go through a major lung operation and bounce back to normalcy in a couple of days? Most importantly, how did my ruptured pancreas get healed without any medication or treatment?

Miraculous, eh? Any doubts? Trust in God and accept the fact that Miracles still do happen, even today and can happen to any one of us.

The truth is, "Everything is possible when God is on our side. He is a true, loving God."

Trust me when I say to you, "God wants each and every one of us by Him. That is where we belong permanently. Everything else that we seek in this world is temporary. "

Inspiration

In conclusion, may I request each and every one of my readers to ask yourself personally, on your own, without the influence of external distractions, being true to your hearts, and knowing that everything is possible, if God is on our side – please ask for yourself, "Am I on God's side? Am I really sincere, true and honest to Him?"

If the answer is 'yes' my dear reader, you have nothing to worry about. The One and Only God Whom I met in heaven is very kind, very loving and a genuine friend. If you are on His side, be rest assured that He will take care of all your needs.

If the answer is 'no' my dear reader, we still can reach God. He wants each and everyone of us to be "on His side" because He still loves us, even if we hate Him. He wants us to become one of His loved ones.

How can we do that? We can come very close to God by simply obeying His five universal instructions that He asked me to write and share with the world.

They are,

1. "Tell the truth."
2. "Commit no more sins."

3. "Surrender yourself completely to God in your daily life."
4. "Walk with God."
5. "Take care of the poor. Open your hearts. Be generous to them. They need your help."

Before I conclude this book, I would like to share one other personal piece of information with my readers. My family physician, Dr. M. D., once asked me in one of my regular visits, "Tell me something. When you were in the hospital, did you have any after life experiences?"

I said, "Yes."

He asked, "Do you mind telling me about it? I am interested to know."

I explained briefly to him how I traveled to an unknown destination with my companion Light; how magnificent was the Kingdom of Heaven; how I discovered the one and only narrow Entry door into Heaven; how and where I met God; His specific instructions to me; etc. etc.

Dr. M. D. said to me that he believed everything I described, because he knew how terrible my condition was and how remarkably I bounced back. "It was amazing!"

I consider myself very fortunate that I was able to see the most beautiful Kingdom of Heaven with my own eyes. I consider myself even more fortunate as I was able to meet God in person and have a heart-to-heart conversation with Him. He sent me back to the earth, and someday, when I complete my unfinished tasks that He assigned to me, I will see Him again.

However, there is one difference in me between last time and my next time. Last time, I was really afraid to die like any one of us. Next time, I am not afraid of death any more. As a matter of fact, I am looking forward to that day when I will see Him again.

May God bless you, my dear reader! Please remember the most important instruction. "Take care of the poor. Open your hearts. Be generous to them. They need your help." In whatever way you can, however you can, please help the needy. In return, God will definitely bestow His blessings many folds on you!

Different Prayers – One Addressee

"Gayatri Mantra"

Om Bhur Bhuvah Swaha
Tat Savitur Varenyam
Bhargo Devasya Dheemahi
Dhiyo yo na - Prachodayat
(Hindu prayer)
I meditate on that great Divine Light
Which enlightens all the three worlds.
May It enlighten me too.

Elohai, n'shama sh'natata bi t'hora hi.

My God, the soul you have placed within me is pure. You breathed of yourself into my flesh, Creating and forming in me a deep awareness of Your Presence. It is you who constantly arouses the desire to live within me. Sometimes you take this hope from me, only to renew it again and again, That I may once more praise you, my God and God of my people. You are the origin of all that happens and every soul is a part of You. Praise are you Eternal One, constantly renewing life within me with your breath of love.

(Jewish Prayer)

We are called in the midst of our lives. Pause a while and know that I am God. We are called to a new way of being in the midst of our ordinary lives and in the midst of our pain. Let be and learn that I am God. Come, let us take time to be still and know. Like a child is quieted at its mother's breast, our souls are calmed and quieted. The still small voice, the calm amidst the storms of our lives, is with us, now and forevermore. We will take time to wait in silence for the Divine Presence from whom our hope comes. Amen.

--From Psalms 49, 62, & 131; I Kings 19:12

Testimonials

READERS' TESTIMONIALS/REVIEWS about Code Blue 99

I am David's mother. David gave me a copy of your book. I was so impressed, I ordered 12 copies to share with my family and friends. I've always been skeptical when reading about these experiences, but your book has really reached out to me. M.S. , Broadview Heights, Ohio

*****

It is the most awesome and interesting book I've ever read! I must also tell you that I cried several times while reading it, and I couldn't wait to meet you. I'm telling all my friends about it, hoping they too will read it.
M.R., Age 12, Parma, Ohio

*****

Insightful - An excellent true short story describing in great detail what awaits us after life on earth. A wonderful read for people of all religions or non-believers. G.C., Bath, Ohio

*****

Fabulous - What a wonderful book! It certainly will inspire you and give you hope for your "future." Read it - you won't regret it – guaranteed
M.N., Broadview Heights, Ohio

*****

Inspirational - This book, Code Blue 99-A Miraculous True Story, is indeed just that, and promises to bring any reader closer to God, as well as provide us with some food for thought regarding what is important while we are living. The author was, in my opinion, chosen by God, to bring this important message to all of us. A wonderful story! Thank you, Sandy Acharjee. E.N., Broadview Heights, Ohio

*****

Humbling and Awe-inspiring Book - Engrossing and awe-inspiring narrative of one person's visit with God. Described in such great detail, and with such conviction, there is little doubt that what he saw and heard is true. It confirms what has been learned in church and is humbling in how little we really know. Mr. Acharjee says he is not a writer, but his writing makes it feel as if he and the reader are sitting together, one-on-one, talking. The story is so engrossing that, once started, it would be very difficult to put it aside. Would be an excellent book for a teenager to read, as well as seniors. It will definitely make the reader pause, think, and, hopefully, act. T.A., Strongsville, Ohio

*****

I have just read your book today, and wanted to let you know how deeply moved I was by it. I first learned of your book on Easter Sunday, as I talked with my brother. My family is facing a difficult time as my elderly mother-in-law suffers from serious illnesses. Your book offered much inspiration. My son, who is only 10, began reading your book yesterday. He is very intrigued by the thoughts you have shared.

I have read/heard of other people that have been clinically dead for a while, later resuscitated in a hospital, and lived to tell about the Light they say they personally experienced. I must admit that in the past, I have viewed such accounts with some skepticism. I don't doubt the sincerity of the authors; but I wondered if they were only dreaming of a Light and Divine Presence as they were physically on the brink between life and death. Yet I've always hoped that God truly exists. After reading your book, I no longer have doubts. Thank you for writing it. M.B., Independence, Ohio

*****

Just finished your book. It was wonderful. Thank you very much. Your faith and conviction in God showed on every page. Because of your book, I feel it's time to know God more. I know He loves me. L.S., Cleveland, Ohio

*****

WOW, I just read your book and your story is truly amazing. I felt many emotions while reading your story and the messages brought back with you; it has really opened my eyes to many things. I have always been a true believer, and I can't wait to share the story with everyone in my life. You are a great man; I have always had the utmost respect for you; I'm sad to hear the details about the pain you and your family experienced throughout the whole ordeal. I am grateful that you are now healthy and that you have such a great story to share about your experiences. God has truly blessed you. G.S., Brecksville, Ohio

*****

Thank you for sending me a copy of your book. As soon as I received the book its cover page impressed me instantly. I read the whole book in one sitting. I must tell you it is a very well written book. The details have touched me. I'm sending you herewith a check for $100. Please donate the additional amount to the needy. It is for a good cause. I wish I could do more. If possible, please send me two more books that I'd like to give them to my family members, one in India and one in France. You are truly a blessed person! T. M., Brantford, Canada

*****

I have read your book while I was traveling by train from Kolkata to Puri. I was extremely amazed to read the contents. I liked the book so much that I'm reading it for the second time. The book is very interesting. If you come to India I want to ask you a few questions in person. It seems to me that you did not write this book for yourself. You wrote it for all of us. Thank you for writing the book. S. A., Kolkata, India

*****

I read your book and I'm absolutely stunned. My elderly father has read the book and he was also stunned. My daughter is currently reading the book and after that my wife wants to read the book. My sister who lives in a distant place wants me to send the book to her. It is absolutely an amazing book and I am telling all my friends to get a copy of the book. Our family is anxiously waiting to meet you in person and hear your experience again from you when you come to India. Please plan to visit us soon. H. G., New Delhi, India

*****

I found the book very interesting. Your donating the money to the needy is very noble. Best wishes. C. M., Brecksville, Ohio

*****

I enjoyed reading your book. I discussed the contents with one of the clergies in our church. You mentioned in the book about the platform or an altar. He said that only the blessed ones are allowed to stand on that platform or altar. You truly are a blessed person. I hope, I too am allowed to stand on that platform when my time comes. I wish your book to be a best seller. D. H., Brecksville, Ohio

*****

I work at an off-shore oil rigging platform in Nigeria with many skilled people primarily from European countries. I was so fascinated after reading your book that I took it to work and shared with many of my colleagues. Someday, I'd like to meet you in person and discuss your experience. R. M., Nigeria, Africa.

*****

All I've heard so far is that you had a near death experience and had a divine encounter of some sort, a visit to heaven where you met God. I am doing some research on this subject at the moment and I am wanting to understand the distinction or difference between the Father, Son and Spirit as God was revealed to you in your experience. Was it as the classical trinity?. Can you give me some explanations on this from what you witnessed or as it was shared. What I am wanting to know is - Is Jesus God or just the Son of God, if so how can Jesus be the Son of God and God at the same time. Also if Jesus is God does this mean Almighty God or is that the Father only, and where does the Holy Spirit come in?. I know of the scriptures in regards to this but I wondered whether your NDE revealed some insight into this. S.C, Perth, Australia

*****

I read your book this weekend, thoroughly enjoyed, and am again so delighted to have met you in person to be a witness to your miracle. Your book was wonderful…I couldn't put it down and plan to pass on to others…of course I will need to buy more copies.

I believe you are a messenger inspired by God. I also know that God has very specific plans for me…and yet I haven't completely figured out what that plan is…other than being a nurse, and being present to give to the poor (mostly emotionally, spiritually, and psychologically as you referred to). I have struggled somewhat with my faith since my son died. D.M., Brecksville, Ohio

*****

The experience that you shared is a miracle, as you have said. It is most evident in the change that has occurred in you, and this cannot happen unless we are transformed by the Lord and surrender to Him. While you were telling me your story, I was marveling, because it was as if you were quoting phrases out of the Holy Bible, which is my frame of reference for faith in God. I have intently studied the writings of the Prophets and Apostles for many years. But yet, if I am correct, you were raised a Hindu and not very familiar with Judaism, Christianity or any such similar writings. This was enlightening to me because you saw what I have read about…G. R., Cleveland, Ohio

*****

I finally just had an opportunity to read the book I purchased from you in October. Don and I are on our way to Florida, and I brought it along, hoping to get a chance to read it. And, I did – out loud, so we were both able to "hear" it. I just had to call you immediately to tell you what a wonderful and moving book it is. My father-in-law is in the hospital with congestive heart failure, and we're going to be seeing him very soon. I am definitely going to tell all our family members and friends about this marvelous book, so they can see for themselves how great it is. Thank you so much for it. J. B., Strongsville, OH

*****

I just finished your book yesterday. It's quite interesting. Overall your book is very impressive. Once it's started to read so it encouraged the readers have to finish the book entirely. After reading this book, I understood that there is someone who control and dictate the entire creatures in a systematic manner. None is super and beyond from HIM. We have to follow HIS commandments all the times. Very few people are lucky like you. The Supreme Power has chosen you to do some important assignment on this planet. Hope you will finish all your remaining work in your new life. If you need any kind of assistance from me to finish your remaining task, please feel free to contact the undersigned. I will do my best that I can..................... God's blessings are always with you to finish your remaining project in your new birth. You will be successful to finish your life mission in this birth under HIS COMMANDMENTS................... R.G., Rexdale, Canada

*****

I found your book so interesting that I read it three times. I found it very inspiring. I still have a few questions that I'd like to ask you in person. Please let me know when you visit Kolkata next time. A. S., Kolkata, India

*****

Such an honor to have met God. In a way, how lucky and proud you must be. You reached out to hundreds or thousands of people like myself to tell your story. How blessed we are to have the computer to communicate with. I gave your story to a friend of mine who happens to also be fascinated with near death experiences. He probably will tell someone else and there you have the ripple effect. You definitely have touched lives with your book. It was as if time stopped and I couldn't stop reading it. For me, it is very hard for me to find a book like yours somewhere. Chris K., Youngstown, OH

*****

I just wanted to write you a note and tell you what a pleasure it was to meet with you on Sunday. I have very much enjoyed your book and completely agree with the five ways you list as ways to grow stronger in our relationship with God.

This week I am visiting friends in North Carolina and I believe your book will be a testimony and a source of inspiration to one of my friends who is doubting the existence of heaven. So once again we experience how God brings God's children together to reach out to someone who is in need of hearing your story in order that they might hear God's story. Thank you for this wonderful ministry

I am already looking forward to your next book. Many blessings, Reverend S.P.+, Brecksville, OH

Author's Email Address: sjs2005@sbcglobal.net